Praise for *On the Other Side of Freedom*

"A poetic, passionate, and deeply personal book."

Washington Post

"An inspiring reminder that hope is vital to any political change, and it's the driving force for any successful attempt at social justice."

Esquire, Best Books of 2018

"Riveting and affecting . . . written with astounding poetry, vulnerability, and flair. Mckesson is a gifted, pointed story-teller."

Village Voice

"By turns lyrical reflection and practical handbook, *On the Other Side of Freedom* reveals the mind and motivations of a young man who has risen to the fore of millennial activism through study, discipline, and conviction. His belief in a world that can be made better, one act at a time, powers his narratives and opens up a view on the costs, consequences, and rewards of leading a movement."

Henry Louis Gates, Jr.

"Hope and insight and empathy spring from every page of *On the Other Side of Freedom*. DeRay Mckesson cools our fears of the struggle, ever guiding us on *how* to struggle. He stares down the faces of bigotry and unfreedom and cynicism and doesn't flinch in writing out our marching orders toward freedom."

Ibram X. Kendi, National Book Award-winning author of *Stamped from the Beginning* and *How to Be an Antiracist*

"From within the heart of the Ferguson protests, DeRay Mckesson writes with a pace you couldn't learn in any writing class. He forces anyone who reads his words to understand the humanity of the black body; the black body that has otherwise been demonised, made monster-like, or contorted into some negative narrative. A vital read, if you are to truly know resistance, and the stories it gives rise to."

Candice Carty-Williams, author of *Queenie*

About the Author

DeRay Mckesson is a civil rights activist, community organizer, and the host of Crooked Media's award-winning podcast, *Pod Save the People*. Spurred by the death of Mike Brown and the subsequent protests in Ferguson, Missouri, and beyond, DeRay has become a key player in the work to confront the systems and structures that have led to the mass incarceration and police killings of black and other minority populations in America. A leading voice in the Black Lives Matter movement and a co-founder of Campaign Zero, DeRay has been praised by President Obama for his work as a community organizer, has advised officials at all levels of government and internationally, spoken at venues from the White House to the Oxford Union, and on TV. Named one of *Time*'s 30 Most Influential People on the Internet and #11 on *Fortune*'s World's Greatest Leaders list, he has received honorary doctorates from The New School and the Maryland Institute College of Art. He lives in Baltimore, Maryland.

@deray
deray.com

ONEWORLD

A Oneworld Book

First published in Great Britain, the Republic of Ireland and Australia
by Oneworld Publications, 2019

ISBN 978-1-78607-651-9
eISBN 978-1-78607-652-6

Typeset design by Meighan Cavanaugh
Printed and bound in Great Britain by Clays Ltd, Elcograf S.p.A.

Oneworld Publications
10 Bloomsbury Street
London WC1B 3SR
England

for you

for all of us

We build our temples for tomorrow, strong as we know how, and we stand on top of the mountain, free within ourselves.

—LANGSTON HUGHES

Contents

Author's Note

Language is the first act. Obvious in retrospect, but something I've had to learn.

I have not always had the words to describe, to unpack, to frame the world around me. None of us have. I have lived more than I can readily process aloud or in text. There are times when the words I have needed have been beyond my reach. Sometimes language is not my friend, not there when I need it, not yet ready to lend a helping hand or a challenge.

There is something unnerving about this reality. It shook me—I started to think that the things I'd lived were not quite real because I did not have the words, the phrases, the stories to convey them in anything beyond my mind. And yet, deep down, I knew that these stories would find life one way or another.

Yet there are other times when the words do come, when I

am able to bring to life the things I've lived, the things I've hoped for and dreamt about, the things that scare me and that bring me joy. And when the words are close, but not ready to peek beyond the surface, not quite the ones we can use to do the work at hand, we are able to create new ones, to make new ways of giving life to the stories of the life we've lived, hoped for, and deserve.

Language, the tool by which power is initially distributed and redistributed: it is in its hands that we find the gateway to liberation, to justice, to freedom. Violence was the first language of this country and is still the first language of many people, but it doesn't have to be the language we teach our children or whose tempo guides our steps. I now know that our stories travel in more than the words we speak or write. Our bodies have carried messages too, of our sorrows and struggles, our demands for the world worthy of our breath, of our happiness and our cool. Our blood has soaked the fields and streets of this country, and it carries reminders of a terror that birthed a nation, destroyed families for generations, and built wealth unlike the world had ever seen. The stories of black folks are etched in the foundation of this America, from its Wall Street to its Market streets, in the buildings of the University of Virginia and Georgetown, in the music that continues to shape culture and society, and in the laws and practices that make the largest institutions sway. In Ferguson too I was reminded that our bodies are communicating as much as our words are, and always have been. That black bodies have always been seen in one way in this world, independent of the words and the noises and the heart.

It is an important part of our work to uncover the stories around us, to understand the messages they carry and use their lessons to guide us in our journey.

We have to name what we fight for, the world we want, a world we have not yet seen. In order to do this well, we have to be able to narrate how we got here, to describe the lives we've lived in order to unearth the things that we may have been too close to understand before. And we have to use our understanding of today to paint a picture of a tomorrow that will shine brighter for those who come behind us.

I have learned too to think more deeply about the words and phrases that we use in the work of social justice to tell stories. I have heard people talk about the importance of community control and community input, but who only believe these things insofar as they get to define exactly who is a part of said community. I have heard people praise a hypothetical community, only to exclude anyone who disagrees with them from their definition of community. Our words and stories must live up to the ideals of the moment in which they are offered. When they do not, the work becomes less about liberation and more about self-service.

I too think every day of the stories that ended too soon, the result of the lives cut before their time. I think of the damage caused by the people who chose to decorate black bodies with bullets instead of love, and how that pain ripples through generations.

This is not the whole story—of my life, of Ferguson, of a movement. I could never tell the whole story of any of those things, as the story is never whole from a single perspective. I can no more tell the story of my growing up, knowing that my sister and my father and my loved ones have their own richness to add, than I can tell the story of the movement or the protests, knowing that all the other people who contributed and participated and were incarcerated have their own perspective to share.

These are the stories that I feel best equipped to tell, having been present in many spaces, in many cities, and experiencing things that I never thought I would, with people I am proud to now call friends and family. These stories are offered in the spirit of protest, in the tradition of those who revealed a part of themselves on paper in hopes that words on paper could help move us closer to justice and equity.

I love my blackness. And yours.

ON THE OTHER SIDE OF FREEDOM

ONE

On Hope

*The impossible is the least that
one can demand.*

—JAMES BALDWIN

I learned hope the hard way.

It was a hot day in St. Louis County in September 2014, and I'd spent the majority of the afternoon sitting on the floor of the St. Louis Metropolitan Police Department headquarters. At nine o'clock in the morning, twenty of us had filed in and plopped down in four rows in the center of the station. The police began to gather around us as hundreds of our fellow protesters turned the corner and were now standing outside the building demanding to get in. When it looked like the officers might forcibly remove us, everyone began to link arms—everyone but me. It was my role to record and interpret as much as possible everywhere we protested so that we could consistently tell the truth to the outside world. So I sat in the front of our stacked rows, unlinked.

I was trying to capture as much as I could on my phone and tweet about it in real time. I wanted to be able to tell the story of the only successful sit-in of a police department since the protests began. We were repeatedly told to move, and we refused. It wasn't long before the officers' growing impatience turned to action. I heard the screaming before I realized that we'd been completely surrounded. It all happened so fast. I looked over and saw a mother trying to stop an officer from driving his thumb into the pressure point behind her daughter's ear. And when I looked up, there was an officer standing directly over me. She told us that we needed to leave immediately. Again, we refused to move. And then she rested her hand on her Taser. I'll never forget how time stopped as I watched her move her hand from her waist to her Taser to her gun, almost like it happened in slow motion.

Suddenly, I was on my back, gliding across the industrial floor as an officer dragged me to the entrance of the building by my ankles. "Why are you doing this?" I asked, as a second officer twisted my arm behind my back. His face fell flat, like he snapped out of the hostility, and instead of a verbal reply, he just let my arm go, picked me up, and pushed me out the door.

It was one of two moments of late when death has felt near. And when death is near, so too is the question of *how: How did I get myself into this situation? Should I have made a different choice?*

—————

I LIVE OFF the beaten path in Baltimore City in a house that people don't wander to. If you come to the house, you have made a decision to be at the house. I've been using ride-sharing apps since I totaled my car in the protests in October 2014, and I was using one on this day in 2017. I saw the car in the driveway, and I paused. But I was already home, so I felt like I had to get out of the car. And when I got out, the driver in the other car got out too. And in that moment, the calmness came over me, like it did in the St. Louis Metro Police Department.

I've received many death threats over the years, the FBI has visited my house, my phone has been hacked, cities have hired surveillance companies that have deemed me a serious threat, and a movie theater was evacuated because I received a threat that I'd be shot during a screening. But none of those things shook me like that day when the car was in front of the house after work.

The driver walked toward me, and I just stood still. I can't even say that I was afraid in that moment. I was still and focused, a stillness and focus that I've known only a few times. I followed his hands and body with my eyes, waiting. Ready. Anxious. He reached out his hand and gave me a packet of papers. I looked down and realized that I'd just been served with a lawsuit. I was sued personally by five police officers:

three in Dallas and two from Baton Rouge. I hadn't been physically served in any of the lawsuits except this one, on the day the guy showed up in my driveway. After he handed me the papers he asked to take a photo, and with that, he was on his way.

These moments forced me to think about the "why" of this work, the fundamental question of whether it is worth the costs. But we all know the risks of protesting, and we choose to meet them head-on. There were so many times in the early months that I was met with an almost paralyzing fear, but as I watched the officer in the police station, I realized that, for what felt like the first time, I wasn't afraid.

It was in losing the fear of death that I began to understand faith and hope.

FAITH IS THE BELIEF that certain outcomes *will* happen and hope the belief that certain outcomes *can* happen. So when Dr. Martin Luther King Jr. says, "The arc of the moral universe is long, but it bends toward justice," he is speaking from a place of faith. He is confident that justice is inevitable even if it may come in another lifetime. Faith is often rooted in the belief in a higher power, in God. Hope, on the other hand, would mean reframing this statement to say, "The arc of the moral universe is long, and it will bend toward justice *if we bend it*." Faith is rooted in certainty; hope is rooted in possibility— and they both require their own different kinds of work.

The work of faith is to actively surrender to forces unseen, to acknowledge that what is desired will come about, but by means that you may never know, and this is difficult. That faith is rooted in certainty does not mean that it never wavers. Indeed, it is not a static belief but one based on trust. And one's trust is not easily conferred.

Hope is the belief that our tomorrows can be better than our todays. Hope is not magic; hope is work. I am not certain that a new world, one of equity and justice, will emerge, but I am certain that it *can* emerge. I have heard people speak of hope in rather different ways. The first is with statements like, "I hope that we win," or "I hope my loved one, diagnosed with incurable cancer, will somehow make it." When we hope in this way, we choose optimism. We believe that perhaps the seemingly extraordinary miracle is within our reach, that it is yet possible. At times, though, when we hope in this manner, we surrender our agency to luck or divine intervention. We acknowledge our limitations in impacting the eventual outcome and rest on optimism as our key act, the primary tool in our toolkit.

When we talk about being hopeful for a future in which black bodies are not considered weapons, it's so easy to deride hope as a platitude, or a nice thought, or even as an enemy of progress. Yet there's another side to hope. Hope can be a driving force. Consider the notion of hope in relation to the way that we use "dream"—a word with a similar dual use. On the one hand, a dream can be the fanciful whimsy of a child, free to explore any one of countless possible realities, completely unmoored from present-day circumstance. But dreams have another, more actionable meaning. Indeed, they can be a firm, dynamic vision of where you want to go. I think this is why we still celebrate the dream of Dr. King, and why parents urge their kids to dream.

Hope is the precursor to strategy. It powers our vision of what roles we must play in bringing about a desired goal, and it amplifies our efforts. I am not surrendering to luck. I am not surrendering to a blind faith that things will just get better. I am reminded that to have faith that a world of equity and justice will emerge does not relinquish one's role in helping it emerge. This is the way to use hope: as faith's companion (and vice versa). When my faith is challenged, it is the belief that things can change that keeps me moving forward. And when hope feels futile, I rely on faith to push forward and help reclaim that certainty.

I have heard critiques of the current wave of activism that are fundamentally critiques of *faith*—there are people deriding this notion that the world *will* be more just and that we *will* end white supremacy. It is those people who look back on the legacy of resistance that we have inherited and challenge its outcomes. The police are still killing people, the argument goes, and the racial wealth gap is as big as it has been since the 1920s. Furthermore, the public education systems have failed black and brown kids throughout the country. Thus the danger in believing in the inevitability of change cannot be overstated. The faith they critique—the belief in unnamed forces that will bring about change—is blind faith, and they are right to be critical. But that is not what animates our striving. Protest is the work of hope. Protest, at its core, is telling the truth in public. It is confrontation and disruption rooted in the acknowledgment of a future that has not yet come, but that is possible. The work at hand is hope-work.

I do not blame anyone who refuses to hold hope in their hands when justice has slipped through our fingers too many times. Many black and other marginalized people have expressed the unfairness of being asked to carry the "burden" of hope, that it's come to feel compulsory for these groups to do so. To this I say that the absence of hope, not its presence, is a burden for people of color. If anything, blackness is a testament of hope: a people born in and of resistance, pushing against a tide meant to destroy, resting in a belief that this world is not the only one that can be.

I think that faith is actually the burden that people have misnamed as the burden of hope. It is not our task to carry the burden of faith, but it is often our choice. My faith wavers often. I and others have fought and lost. I have seen people crushed by the weight of the opposition. I have seen the best of intentions transformed into self-interest or terror. And I have seen optimism blind people and keep them from addressing the realities of the horror they face. But when my faith wavers, my hope carries me through.

I think that in some ways the hope of black people is the

fuel for this nation; that it is the creativity and ingenuity of a people who have had every reason to choose resignation but have not that fuels both the culture and cadence of this American life.

FREEDOM IS NOT only the absence of oppression, but is also the presence of justice and joy. We are fighting to bring about a world that we have not seen before. "Make America Great Again" is a familiar evocation of a mythical time of human flourishing in our nation's history. What is posited as a time of "greatness" was, for many, a time of rampant racism, xenophobia, misogyny, and sexism. We have never seen a world of equity, justice, and joy. We are trying to create something altogether new. And it is impossible to create something new in the absence of hope.

I would even go so far as to say that many who decry hope the loudest could eventually be the most hopeful among us. They are doing the pre-work of hope, deconstructing our current realities. But they are afraid that they may fail, so they hesitate to build. Or they fear that the work will be so long-term that it will result in disappointment—and they are trying to guard against disappointment—so they challenge. They explore and unpack but are slow to create. And they publicly decry any efforts to bring forth a better world, because of the possibility and weight of disappointment. To them it sounds fluffy and hollow.

But a belief in tomorrow has never been hollow. It wasn't hollow to those who fought before us. We do not stand in the shadows of those who came before us, but in their glow. And that glow exists because they put forth a vision of the future and they fought for it. We did not invent resistance or discover injustice in August 2014. We exist in a legacy of struggle, a legacy rooted in hope.

We have a hope rooted in a belief that as sure as hands have made the buildings that dominate the skylines of our cities, hands have made the institutions, practices, and customs that perpetuate racism and injustice that permeate those same cities. What is made by human hands requires maintenance. Buildings can be torn down and built over. Parking lots can become parks and vice versa. Institutions can evolve, change, or be dismantled.

We can win. And if we do, it will be because more of us understood that this is a system of choices, and we have learned how to build power to make new choices. When they say that power concedes nothing without a demand, they are reminding us that the demand has to create something new— a new power dynamic, a new reality. And hope is the fuel of this demand.

Hope is not magic. Hope is work. Let's get to the work.

TWO

How Am I Supposed to Respond to Murder?

When you know your name, you should hang on to it, for unless it is noted down and remembered, it will die when you do.

—TONI MORRISON

I
t was illegal to stand still on the streets of Ferguson, Missouri, in August, September, and October 2014. This wasn't on account of any law that had existed prior to the presence of hundreds and thousands of protesters in the streets; it wasn't on account of any law at all. It was a rule, if one could even call it that, born of hubris and desperation. The police were simply out of ideas for how to coax the swelling ranks of protesters out of the streets. So they thought they'd wear us out. And before we knew it, we were walking, day and night.

It became known as the Five-Second rule: Anyone who stood still for more than five seconds was arrested. Being forced to walk day and night is one of the things I will never forget, a reminder that the law in practice is never neutral, that it can change at the whim of those in power, and that the battles our elders fought are not as far behind us as we had been raised to believe. In the courthouse in downtown St. Louis, there are images of Lady Liberty, but I know that justice is not blind; she chooses not to see my humanity.

Days before the Five-Second rule, Governor Jay Nixon of Missouri, in a news conference, imposed a midnight curfew that he claimed was "not to silence the people of Ferguson, but to address those who are drowning out the voice of the people with their actions." State Highway Patrol Commander Captain Ronald S. Johnson subsequently declared, "We won't enforce it with trucks, we won't enforce it with tear gas, we will enforce it with communication. . . . We will be telling the people, 'It's time to go home.'"

On the first night of the citywide midnight curfew in Ferguson, the tear gas began at eight o'clock.

Before we ever saw or felt it, we heard the sound of the canister leaving the barrel of the gun—a sound between a large firework and a cartoon cannon—followed by a whiz as it moved through the air. My most vivid memory of that night was seeing a child, maybe five years old, frantically running, directionless and alone. He seemed to notice first what I only realized moments later—that two canisters had fallen near us. By the time I saw that he was crying, he was swept up by a parent and I was stuck in a cloud. I tried to outrun the tear gas but I was surrounded—there were cars behind me, a gate to my side, and the gas was moving quickly. This was not the scene I'd envisioned just one day ago when I arrived.

The afternoon before, I had prepared for this. I'd been at another protester's house for the first training led by the street medics—current and former medical professionals—who had just arrived in Ferguson. Street medics assist activists in protest since ambulances rarely, if ever, visit active protest sites. I had never even thought about such a team of people existing, let alone that I'd be in one of their training sessions. And yet there I was, one of eight people spending the better part of an afternoon learning how to flush my eyes out in the event of being teargassed and how to properly assist those around me in distress. I first met Alexis Templeton and Johnetta Elzie at that training; they were two St. Louis natives whose lives would intertwine with mine in unexpected ways over the following days and then months and then years. But we were just getting to know one another then, and none of us had expected to make use of this information so soon. We were told that tear gas can sear your contacts to your eyes—I considered removing mine, but in the end decided not to. Not twenty-four hours later, I was putting my head in my shirt and running through smoke.

When I got through to the other side of the smoke, I uncovered my head and was thankful that I could still see. I didn't have more than a few seconds to consider my sight before I was swept up in a cloud of protesters, all of us seemingly running for our lives. I felt like my life was hanging in the balance and time was standing still. The police, armed with rubber bullets, were in SWAT vehicles chasing us up West

Florissant Avenue, the main site of the protests. They drove us in every direction, in their supposed effort to clear the street.

It was like we were being hunted.

Hours later, SWAT vehicles drove down the streets while officers hung off them, shining flashlights into cars. They were still looking to round us up. I'd eventually made it back to my car on the side street where I'd parked it. I knew that I'd have to drive down West Florissant to get to where I was sleeping that night, but my only instinct was to hide. I was sitting with the lights off when it clicked: in that moment, on Nesbit Drive, I couldn't be in my car. I couldn't be on that street. I made myself as small as possible, hiding under my steering wheel, praying that the light wouldn't expose me. It would be hours before I finally drove away.

Days later, I'd be out in the streets again, and four police officers would inform me that I was walking too slowly; that I could not pace back and forth in a given area; that standing still was now illegal.* Even the reporters had to walk, either because the police forced them to, or because we the protesters demanded it: "You don't get to come down here and watch us like animals," one protester yelled to a reporter, "you've gotta keep it moving too, or you've gotta go." They would not simply be voyeurs of our pain. And that particular reporter got the message. He walked.

---

* I tweeted about this encounter and, as it was the first public record of the Five-Second rule, it was later used in the court case *Abdullah v. County of Saint Louis, Missouri et al* that resulted in the practice being declared unconstitutional.

Those of us who were there remember the Five-Second rule as a defining characteristic of the beginning of this movement. We remember adapting to it and meeting it as a challenge. Instead of tiring us out, it only firmed our resolve. We couldn't stand still? Okay. We would march all day and all night, and we would make the police do the same. We wouldn't be the only people exhausted, we reminded them.

I often wondered where was this "nation of laws" that was so often invoked in political discourse, when it was so easy for the police to unilaterally create and enforce a set of rules in the name of public safety. Why was it so easy for them to obscure the reality of why we were in the streets in the first place?

I've read stories about search parties rounding up black men and women. I've seen the photos of protesters bloodied for daring to march in politically inconvenient places. But I never thought that in an American city in 2014 it would be illegal to stand still. I never thought I'd have to hide under my steering wheel to escape the police. I never thought I'd learn to maneuver in tear gas like I learned how to tie my shoes, awkwardly and slowly at first and then with grace. It wasn't that I thought America was better than teargassing its own citizens—I knew that was not so. But I thought those tactics were a thing of the past. Instead, the default reaction to black bodies assembled in protest was to treat us as a threat.

WHAT IT'S TAUGHT ME is that freedom is fragile, and that's a lesson that I never want to forget.

Indeed, it's something I actively try to remember. It's the reason that I still wear my blue Patagonia down vest. We were in the street for four hundred days, through all four seasons. And during the first winter, I needed something to wear that would keep me warm, but that I'd never have to pack. That was when I started wearing the vest. It was simple, warm, and never felt bulky. When the weather got cold, I'd just put a hoodie under it. I got used to wearing it, like a safety blanket of sorts. But it also serves as a reminder. I've worn it every day since the winter of 2014. I had it on when we got pepper sprayed, smoke bombed, and shot at with rubber bullets in Ferguson, in Baltimore, in Charleston, and in every city I was invited to after the initial wave of protests ended. It may seem silly, but it keeps me grounded in the reality of all that has happened.

And that specific reality is all the more important as accounts of the days and months following the Ferguson protests are told, as the *history* of this movement is penned. Already the story has been framed and retold by people who were not a sustained presence either in person or virtually before the movement became popular, before we'd built the critical mass of supporters across the world. And it is being taken over either to stand in for a range of intellectual experiences or to reinforce particular narratives that fit personal ends. I think this may be a danger of the internet, of feigned proximity.

But those of us who were there, we remember. We remember how quickly the safe houses were established, how smoothly the bail fund operated. We remember the lawyers, like the ArchCity Defenders and the legal observers, who set up clinics to close active warrants of protesters, and the dinners by Cathy Daniels, affectionately called Mama Cat, who served us meals—at times our only meals—in all types of weather and tense moments. We remember Johnetta Elzie collecting supplies at the QuikTrip, before she and I began to work on the daily newsletter together, along with Brittany Packnett. And Tef Poe leading the long marches from West Florissant to the Ferguson Police Department headquarters.

We remember Tony Rice and others holding down the fort in the white tent at Andy Wurm's lot across from the Ferguson Police Department, and The Lost Voices becoming an active group within the larger protest community. We remember Tribe X planning and executing the first mall shutdowns. And the old Ferguson Burger Bar, which fed us when every other place seemed too afraid to stay open. I especially remember all the donations of water in those first hundred days, how supporters would order pizza online and have it delivered to places close to where we were.

I remember too all the people that told us that protest was not the way to make a difference, that we were wasting our time, that we needed to try different methods that were more acceptable. When the protests began, I still worked for Minneapolis Public Schools. The steady stream of hate calls I began to receive—and the flood of complaints that members of the Board of Education were receiving—forced us to remove everyone's office phone number from the Minneapolis Public Schools' Human Capital website. Today, people talk about the protests as an important part of the ecosystem of citizenship, but that was not the case in the beginning.

On most nights, I slept on couches, floors, or air mattresses of either old friends I had known in college who happened to live in St. Louis, or new friends I had met in the streets. I think of the protests in two waves: before the nonindictment of Michael Brown Jr.'s killer, Darren Wilson, and after. Before the decision, there was a persistent on-edge feeling: We never knew when the decision would come, but we knew that if it was indeed a nonindictment that the protests would look like something we hadn't seen yet. Every day it seemed we'd hear rumors and get texts that "today was the day." And when the day finally came, that night was a night unlike all the rest. Police cars burned; tear gas dissolved in the air in clouds so thick and indistinguishable from all the other smoke that you didn't realize what it was until you couldn't breathe. And then there was the National Guard, strewn throughout the area, hiding on main roads behind buildings, ready for action.

We remember because we learned so much about ourselves in the process, about organizing, about police violence, about liberation beyond survival, and about the difference between

the people willing to talk about resistance and the people willing to do the work of resistance.

We did not know many things in those early days, but we
knew a few things well: that Michael Brown Jr. should be alive
and that we would not and could not leave the streets. And so
we stayed, all night, every night, confident that we were on
the right side of justice. And knowing these things was the
fuel that led us to stand firm despite, or perhaps because of,
the terror that the police were inflicting on us. We may not
have known each other's names, but we knew each other's
hearts. And it was not that we were not afraid—often we were.
But we had known fear in our silence too. And we had grown
tired of being silent.

> *Indict! Convict! Send that killer cop to jail!*
> *The whole damn system is guilty as hell!*

> *They say move back, we say fight back.*
> *Call: Move back. Response: Fight back.*

WHEN A MESSAGE is spoken loud and clear and in unison
when formerly there were whispers or collections of disparate
rumblings, it's easy to think of people as finally having found
their voices, as if those voices had been lost. That they are
being heard now, though, is an indictment of the listener, not

the speaker. We the protesters have never been the voiceless. We have been the unheard. Our storytelling has been key to our survival, as we have spoken about our pain and our joy, even if we were talking to ourselves.

It is common since the protests began to hear people, confused about our tactics, ask: Why are you doing this? Why are you demanding, now, to be heard?

Protest is telling the truth in public. Sometimes protest is telling the truth to a public that isn't quite ready to hear it. Protest is, in its own way, a storytelling. We use our bodies, our words, our art, and our sounds both to tell the truth about the pain that we endure and to demand the justice that we know is possible. It is meant to build a community and to force a response.

We would never have gone into the streets if Michael Brown Jr. hadn't been killed. Or if thousands hadn't been killed before him. The protesters in Minneapolis would not have barricaded the Fourth Precinct police station if Jamar Clark hadn't been killed, if Rekia Boyd hadn't been killed as she walked, if Aiyana Jones hadn't been asleep on her couch and shot through the wall by an officer, or if Philando Castile hadn't been slain while complying with every request and command from the officer who shot him. We took to the streets as a matter of life and death. What else could we do?

How, exactly, are we supposed to respond to murder?

It seems we have two options: We can accept the trauma and go about our daily lives—carry the weight of the violence inflicted upon us and pray that we survive. And if we choose to accept it, to suffocate in surrender, then we must ask ourselves, What kind of life is possible in surrender?

Or we can challenge the source of the trauma. We can resist. And if we choose to resist, we must ask ourselves, How do we resist and to what end?

On the streets in Ferguson, and in all the days since, a generation has chosen the latter. We choose to challenge the trauma, and though we know that it won't be easy, we know that the alternative is impossible, for we have already lived through the suffocating reality of silence. When Trayvon Martin was killed, we watched in real-time disbelief as the system let his killer go and itself remained relatively unchanged. Florida's Stand Your Ground law became just another way to justify a modern-day lynching. By the time Michael Brown Jr. was killed two years later, we knew all too well that we were not promised a better tomorrow, but that we would have to force one into existence.

My generation grew up with the message of progress. Our elders speak of how far we've come, that our worst days are behind us. Indeed, that the moral distance we've traveled from enslavement to Jim Crow to today is unfathomable. That just a half century ago, it would have been hard to imagine the freedoms that we now have, and thus progress, it would seem, is inevitable.

The history lessons we learned in school were always ones of struggle and *accomplishment*—our freedom gained,

Constitution changed, national holidays proclaimed, and so on. But when Michael Brown Jr.'s body lay in the street, the latest death in what was becoming a public record of indiscriminate kills by the police, the notion of accomplishment rang hollow. And so we could not remain silent. A response to murder that involves silence only invites more murder. We could not afford to surrender to the faith in a better tomorrow.

We chose protest as a matter of survival.

To challenge the source of the trauma offered us, and still offers us, the best chance at a world that we deserve. In making that choice toward challenge and away from surrender, we—I—assert that as sure as there is nothing inevitable about progress toward justice, there is no immutable permanence to injustice. Our ability to choose implies a latent power that is seldom used to its full extent. When we talk about power in the context of protest, we often talk about "empowering" others, as if power is like a bag of candy that one can dole out at will. But one can neither give nor be given power; we can only help one another stand in our own power.

When we protest, we are simply individuals coming together to use power and activate hope. I have yet to meet a protester rallying against a reality that she didn't think she could change. And from those first days in Ferguson to now, that is what the protests have done all over the country and all over the world. People have been reminded that they have power, that they must stand in that power, and that when they do, they can change the world. But working for change implies a freedom to look toward the future, a freedom scarcely experienced by people consumed by the pressing concerns of daily life. I know what it's like to be so overwhelmed.

I grew up in a community of recovery—both of my parents had once been addicted to drugs, my mother left when I was three years old, and my father raised me and my sister. We slept on the floor when gunshots got too close to the house, thinking that it would be harder for a bullet to pierce the floorboards than the window or wall. Of my four aunts and uncles, only one ever had schooling past high school, and neither of my parents did. We were not quite middle class but lived a life that shielded us from aspects of the reality of our poverty. I never imagined a world outside of Baltimore, not because I lacked a rich imagination but because Baltimore was the only world I'd ever known other than what was on TV. As an adult, I now realize that I had only seen the majority black parts of Baltimore, which happened also to be the lower-income parts; I didn't know that affluent neighborhoods like Homeland or Canton even existed. I could not name mass incarceration, the racial wealth gap, or describe food deserts until recently. It wasn't that I hadn't seen the impact of these things in my life growing up. I had. But to me they were not phenomena to be named, studied, and "reformed"; they were simply the way the world was.

Only through exposure would I learn to see the world differently, and thus gain the tools I needed to broaden my perspective. A white water rafting trip in college provided one such opportunity. The trip was designed to help train me and others for our roles on the Residential Life staff. I'll never forget it because I fell off the raft and got trapped in the current. In that moment, I thought I was going to die. I can swim, but if you've ever been caught in a current, you know that it's hard for even the best swimmers to escape its wrath. All that I could think about was my next breath—I wasn't thinking about my sister, my father, my hopes and dreams. I just wanted to breathe freely again. I realized that this is what being in proximity to trauma sometimes does to us—it traps us in the current, in the present.

Too many of us are forced to think about life from the vantage point of the current, and thus it's tempting to accept trauma as a condition of the world we live in. This is not because we lack hope, but because our hope has not yet been activated. We are, after all, inundated with images of injustice and atrocities daily. Life goes on, as they say. Doing anything more than coping can seem too great a task when there are bills to be paid or family to be taken care of. But to accept trauma as a condition of this world is to surrender both our imagination of what tomorrow could look like and our agency in actively shaping what today feels like. Make no mistake, our world, our experience, is changing constantly. When we surrender, we leave it to others to define what that change looks like. History has shown us the consequences of inaction. We can and should acknowledge the trauma that we face, but

———

we should not accept it. Indeed, we cannot fight what we do not name, so name it we must, but we can never accept it. We will never get to the other side of freedom if we accept the trauma as a feature and not a flaw of this world.

THERE'S A DOUBLE STANDARD to protest in America. Something is different for black people who should dare to ask questions, and further, for those who protest in blackness. Protest in and by black bodies is never deemed legitimate, never deemed worthy of engagement. It seems that we have simply not earned our right to grievance yet. And because we have not earned our grievance, our grievance is illegitimate— we do not deserve sympathy or, ultimately, justice.

This is a familiar mode of reasoning. There is an earn/ deserve paradigm when it comes to resource allocation, and it determines the degree to which one is worthy of a service, a good, of power, or of life. It is a commonly held belief that people of color or poor people have not actually earned health care, housing, access to equitably funded public education, and so forth. To the contrary, the attainment of these things, the argument goes, is a function of effort, or intelligence, or decision-making—all things that these groups supposedly lack. On the flip side, those who already have health care, or housing, or access to equitably funded public education believe that they earned these things, and should they somehow find themselves lacking, that they have a case for intervention.

Racism, the belief that one race is inherently less valuable than others, is rooted in an imbalance of power. In terms of the earn/deserve paradigm, racism dictates that a set of people, defined by race, are simply less worthy, regardless of individual or collective effort, and that there is no set of actions that could actually make them worthy, because the bar is always moving. Conversely, white people are inherently worthy; they have obviously done the work of earning and therefore are entitled to resources, opportunities, and life.

The reality is that human flourishing is a more complicated function of effort, circumstance, and luck, among other things. But regardless, what we find with race is that people of color are deemed as high need-to-earn and low deserve, while white people are high deserve and low need-to-earn. The closer one's proximity to power, the greater one's sense of entitlement to that power.

There was a time when I believed that racism was rooted in self-interest or economics—the notion that white supremacy emerged as a set of ideas to codify practices rooted in profit. I now believe that the foundation of white supremacy rests in a preoccupation with dominance at the expense of others, and that the self-interest and economic benefits are a result, not a reason or cause. I believe this because of the way that white supremacy still proliferates in contexts where there is no self-interest other than the maintenance of power. I have seen it hold sway even in contexts where it does not materially benefit the white people who hold the beliefs.

I've been in hundreds of meetings about pathways to change over the past three years, and I've come to realize that the earn/deserve paradigm is potent and pervasive, and that it is the prism through which much of our media does its reporting and the bedrock of our leaders' policymaking.

WALTER SCOTT WAS KILLED by Officer Michael Slager in North Charleston, South Carolina, in 2015. He was shot in the back while running away from the officer. Later, Slager lied about the event, claiming that Scott had reached for his gun, thus causing the officer to fear for his own life. Video evidence captured by a bystander proved Slager a liar, and he was later convicted of murder. But these facts were somehow not always salient to the local media. I was in South Carolina on the day of Walter Scott's funeral, and I remember standing outside the funeral home after the service when the front page of the *Post and Courier,* the largest newspaper in South Carolina, caught my eye with the following headline: WHEN YOU'RE BEHIND, YOU'RE BEHIND. LIKE MANY DOGGED BY MOUNTING CHILD-SUPPORT DEBT, WALTER SCOTT FACED AN

ARDUOUS FUTURE, LIKELY JAIL TIME.[*] Now, one can read this and not realize that Walter Scott was the victim. But anyone with even the basic facts of the case would certainly question how this newspaper could have framed the event in terms so divorced from reality. Of course, if you think that Walter Scott could have, perhaps should have, made different life choices, and that these different life choices would have saved his life in the end, then this framing makes sense.

The headline shifts culpability from the officer who used deadly force on an innocent man and places it on Walter Scott, the unarmed man, the victim. It is as if Scott's case, which by then had clear evidence that he was shot in the back as he ran away, was still being contested. That is the earn/deserve paradigm at work in the media.

Notably, this line of thinking is not simply confined to issues of policing or media representation. Public education is another area where clearly we see this logic function to devastating effect. Take Baltimore City Public Schools in my home state. Over 90 percent of students are black and Latino, 90 percent of students live in poverty, and the school system has the highest percentage of special education students in the state. In defending the inequity of resource allocations to the school system, the governor of Maryland has made the following statements: "This may be the most highly funded school

---

[*] The *Post and Courier* has since changed the title of this article on its website, but the original title can be found on www.pulitzer.org.

system in America" and "Maryland spends more than twice as much in Baltimore City as we do in the rest of the state." That Baltimore City is one of the highest-funded school systems in the state of Maryland is patently false. The state funding formula that the governor's statement is based on in fact uses a regressive property tax that disadvantages Baltimore, a city with a poor population. This is just one example, but one that might find echoes in other states across the country.

Why wouldn't we simply allocate whatever resources we need to ensure that our kids have a great education? Because they are black and brown and the subtext is that they have not yet earned a sufficient investment. We must ask, What would they need to do though in order to prove that they are worthy of additional resources?

How does one respond to an ideology that does not deem you worthy of basic necessities like food, water, shelter, even life?

ON AUGUST 14, 2014, we stood in the largest meeting room of the Urban League Building in Minneapolis, about a hundred or so people, waiting for the conference call to begin. I was sweating a little, a combination of my nerves and the weather. Somehow, I was on red-ribbon duty, tying red ribbons around everyone's wrists in an act of solidarity for the call.

Then the call started, with people from all over the world participating. We had a moment of silence for the life and death of Michael Brown Jr. and other victims of police violence. It was heavy. It always feels heavy when we talk about death, regardless of how many times we've discussed it. I left the moment of silence and stood in front of the Fourth Precinct police station, holding a sign in protest so that drivers could see it as they rode down the street. This was the same precinct that protesters would barricade and shut down in memory of Jamar Clark two years later.

I felt like I had done something, that I had done my part, perhaps, by attending the National Moment of Silence. I didn't know at the time, but I was in just one of 114 cities that participated in the National Moment of Silence organized by @FeministaJones via Twitter. I'd never been in a room of strangers with a shared purpose like that before. So many people coming together because a kid got killed. And somehow it didn't feel like enough to me, though I didn't know what *more* looked like.

Years earlier I taught sixth-grade math in Starrett City, the largest federally funded housing projects in the country, in Brooklyn, New York. Teaching is the most important thing that I've ever done. And it was there that I started thinking more about ensuring that the commitments I made were living commitments.

As a teacher, I was always frustrated by people, many of them fellow teachers, who proclaimed they stood with and would fight for our students but who never put those ideas into action. We'd be in professional development sessions and educators would say things about our kids and their families that would never be acceptable in mixed company. And when confronted about their tone, they'd scoff and assert that their comments weren't representative of their true feelings, because, look, they were teachers!

I found myself thinking more and more about what it would mean to do my part.

I was living in Minneapolis at the time and working as the senior director of Human Capital for Minneapolis Public Schools, a role similar to the one I'd held previously in Baltimore. I was responsible for all staffing in the district—from hiring to salary setting. School systems hire the majority of staff during the summer, so by August I was busy at work and that was pretty much my life.

But I needed to do more.

I had a one-bedroom apartment in downtown Minneapolis, and most nights I slept on the couch with the TV on. Late on August 15, 2014, I was watching the news and saw the protests unfold, and then I checked my phone and saw the conversation on Twitter. On TV, it looked like the protesters were angry and unruly. On Twitter, it looked like the police were out of control and reckless. I wanted to see what was happening with my own eyes.

My best friend, Donnie, had recently gotten married, and part of our unspoken deal was that I wouldn't call him in the middle of the night unless there was an emergency. I had a tendency to call before realizing what time it was, and I didn't want to be that friend who called at all hours of the night. It was 2:00 A.M. Saturday when I made the decision to go to

Ferguson, and I felt like I needed to tell someone before I drove nine hours to a place I'd never been before. I couldn't call my father; he'd definitely say no. I could possibly call TeRay, my sister, but it would be fifty-fifty. So I just waited until 8:00 A.M., when it'd be okay to call Donnie.

"I think I'm going to go to Ferguson. Now. What do you think?" I said to him when he answered. "If you think you should go, you should go," he replied. By then, I'd already packed a bag and was standing in the doorway, just waiting for someone I trusted to tell me that I wasn't losing my mind. I was about four hours into the drive to Missouri when I posted the following Facebook status:

> Almost in Ferguson, MO. Any friends (or friends-of-friends) in St. Louis with a spare couch I can crash on for a few days?

I had faith that I'd know someone who at least knew someone else with a couch I could sleep on. I'd never been to Missouri before so I didn't have any connections that I knew personally. Shortly after posting this, I got a call from Jessica Cordova Kramer, a former colleague, who told me that she'd reached out to one of her friends, Brittany Packnett, who found a place for me to stay for at least the first night.

When I arrived in St. Louis, I went to Brittany's friend's house, dropped off my bag, and went to the streets. I didn't bring a lot with me as I'd only planned to be in Ferguson for the weekend. At that point, I had only understood the protests from Twitter and TV.

I didn't realize that we'd be in the streets for over a year. On the second night, I was teargassed for the first time. And by day four, my legs were wearying from the walking.

Joining the protest changed so much. It only took those first two days for me to realize that I'd stay longer than a weekend—indeed, that I'd stay in the streets for as long as it took. I called out from work, stayed the next week, then traveled the nine hours to and from my home in Minneapolis until I eventually quit my job and moved to St. Louis County permanently.

I'm not from St. Louis, but I came to know it as well as I would a second home. I know it by the places we shut down, by the police departments we challenged, by the terrain of protest. It is a city with a spirit and resolve that stands apart.

THREE

The Problem of the Police

day, though, the fear came later. As the ev
like I was the sixth-grade math teach
ing to talk one of my students
calm, steady tone to mask
yell back, that an es
that I couldn't
possible w
silenc

I could feel t[...] [...]ar and power in his voice, on[...] [...]e tension in his arm as he steadied his gu[..], pointing it at my face and then torso, yelling and cursing. I just remember fragments of his rage as he barked, "Put your fucking hands on the steering wheel," and when I complied, he continued, "What the fuck were you doing?" He was young—likely my age, or slightly older, both of us just having entered adulthood, wearing it now like an ill-fitting jacket. The sun hadn't yet broken through the sky, and dew was still on my windshield. I lived around the corner and hadn't made it far before his flashing lights appeared.

"It'll be okay," I said to him in a low, level tone, repeatedly, as he approached the driver's-side window where I sat. Sometimes fear is a luxury, the by-product of having the time and space to process, to consider options and alternatives. On that

nts unfolded, I felt

er that I used to be, try-

own from a tantrum, using a

my emotion. I knew that I couldn't

alation would certainly end in disaster,

xit the car, and that no phone call would be

ile his gun was pointed at me. And I sensed that

e wouldn't work in my favor either. The officer yelled and cursed as he approached my window for reasons I don't think either of us knew, and as he carried on, the only words that found their way to my lips were, "It'll be okay," over and over. It was all that I could think of to make the situation less tense—to calm his frenzy. I think it just wasn't my time to leave this earth, because it worked. He lowered the gun, he gave me neither a ticket nor a warning, he simply got back in his car and drove away.

Later, I called a former mentor and friend who worked in the Baltimore City State's Attorney's Office and told her what happened. I asked her how to report it, and she told me to let it go and to be more careful next time. I did as she said. That was in 2009.

Conflict exists in community. And not all conflict is the same; it has dimensions, nuance. If we are to live in community with each other, we must acknowledge this reality. Living in community requires a shared set of values and norms to serve as guideposts, defining the behaviors that we want to encourage and discourage, outlining the actions that make our community stronger and those that take away from its strength. In effect, we have rules for dealing with conflict. It is in this context that we understand that the choice to live among others requires the presence of a mechanism for responding to conflict, to instances when norms and values are broken or alleged to have been broken. But the choice to live in community also means that the community must dictate those norms and values for itself and must be able to manage the set of interventions used when conflict inevitably arises.

In ways large and small, we cede aspects of individual autonomy when we choose to live with one another. From the stop signs and traffic lights that create order on our roads, to trusting the FDA to ensure that the foods we eat are safe, we acknowledge that there are some things that individuals should not be able to decide on their own, as the impact on the larger community is too great.

CHIEF IN OUR DESIRE for a well-functioning community is, among other things, the desire that order be preserved, that conflicts be managed in ways that both make us safe and make us *feel* safe. No one wants disorder or chaos—not in their home, not in their neighborhood, not in their life. Sometimes, though, the compromises we make to purportedly keep order imperil us in unexpected ways. This is true of the way that our desire for safety has manifested. In a cruel twist, it has led us to make sacrifices that make us less safe, that increase the conflicts in our communities, and that empower a set of citizens to create conflict with impunity.

And it is our desire for safety, combined with measures for conflict management that prize the whims of the most privileged among us, that have led us to the state of policing in this country today.

The police in America have positioned themselves to be the first defense in addressing conflict. And that evolution has coincided with the fact that conflict is treated uniformly for people of color and other marginalized groups, while conflict is treated with nuance for white people. In theory, the police are the neutral party that responds to conflicts. But power, especially unchecked power, is never neutral. We know that the police function altogether differently depending on who you are or where you come from. The theory of policing is quite far from the reality of policing. For us, at least, that is.

They primarily wield negative power—that is, they take away to purportedly give. They seize, detain, arrest, imprison, and kill to maintain law and order in society, in order to manage conflict. What does it mean that the institution we've created to respond to conflict primarily uses means that are expressly for destruction and not for building? They do nothing to equip people with tools and resources to make better choices in the future, to learn how to manage conflict in the absence of intervention, to understand how their decisions impact the larger society.

Some people would argue that this is not their role. And

given the way they have been allowed to function to date, these people are right. From movies to TV shows, to stump speeches and rallies, they have come to convince society that the only way to ensure safety is to employ negative power with both discretion and impunity. But we know that this does not increase the reality of safety, even if it increases the perception of safety. In many ways, the police are the gateway into the larger system of incarceration. They are not arbiters, they are ushers, shepherding men and women, and increasingly children, into subjection.

It is the people on the margins who are most aware of the dissonance between the theory and practice of the police and policing. There are three reasons for this: first, because they have intimate knowledge of the difference between conflicts of survival and conflicts of choice, and of how the police respond to both; second, because they have endured the presence of negative power as a means of control in the name of order, stability, and community for ages; and last, because they know that their instances of conflict in community almost always involve the weight of the police, whereas those of other members of the community, namely those who are white, do not.

Conflicts of survival arise as a result of the conditions created by the inequity in society, conditions like poverty and its concentration, mass incarceration, mass supervision, or the structural lack of access. This is not to excuse any range of conflicts that arise as a result of personal failures in judgment, but to note that some are a result of choices that have been made or allowed at the structural level. So there are high amounts of reported theft in places where poverty is the most stark, high levels of drug use and distribution in places where poverty and incarceration coincide, gun crimes in communities of densely concentrated poverty, and assaults in places where the traditional justice system has failed and a system of street justice is all anyone knows.

Conflicts of choice are those that are primarily the result of the personal decisions of an individual and not the result of systemic failures resulting in inequity. These are things like tax fraud, domestic abuse, insider trading, arson, embezzlement.

As a society, we have control over the conditions that lead to the conflicts of survival. And as a society, we have largely made the choice that we will allow them to continue. We could choose to end poverty; end homelessness; develop a robust program for addressing mental illness; guarantee that every adult and child has food and shelter; and institute a living wage and work opportunities for everyone. We could make these choices at a much larger scale in society. But we choose not to.

The consolidation of negative power, especially with no oversight or accountability, is the gateway to totalitarianism. Communities of color and marginalized communities have experienced the realities of how the heavy presence of negative power can fundamentally alter life forever. We're increasingly seeing unrest that either begins with police violence or is sustained because of the absence of the police. It is important to remember that this negative power is not used in white communities with as much frequency or with the same intensity that it is used in communities of color. And this matters, because white people experience a host of diversion programs and their like when they engage in similar types of conflict. We also see the police create a conflict in order to then solve the conflict—the escalation of conflicts involving actors with mental illness is a ready example of this.

Will we always need a response to conflict? Yes. Do we need the police as they currently exist? No. It is not simply that policing is broken. This isn't like a toy. Policing isn't something to be bandaged up and fixed. The institution of policing is built on an overly simplistic understanding of conflict, flawed assumptions about reducing conflict over time, and a denial of the way that structural bias influences the way conflict is addressed. Policing as we know it is the wrong response to the challenges of conflict that we experience in communities. I think of policing today as a drinking glass with holes in it. No matter how many times you plug a hole here, mend one there, water continues to leak. At some point, you need to acknowledge the glass is faulty. That's policing.

Importantly, the problem is not limited to a few bad apples, but rather a bad barrel—today's culture of policing simply doesn't match the needs of communities.

It's also not a matter of a bad policeman or good policeman. Indeed, this is not about individual people. It's about a system, an institution, that is responding in ways that don't actually make sense for the people they purport to serve. We hear the police tout the notion of being a guardian or a warrior in communities. But we don't need guardians if the guardians kill us, and we don't need warriors at war with the people needing protection.

We have been convinced that we will not know safety if we do not know the police. But says who? They are the thin line between a complete overhaul of the system and a tinkering at the edges of the status quo. And this is why people double down on their power. But we must be able to conceive of another way to respond to conflict that is not rooted in negative power—we have done it elsewhere, in homes, in classrooms, in communities. We have seen models of restorative justice, in which communities manage conflicts that arise among themselves, without needing the intervention of a government agency. We have to be honest and imaginative about where we are and where we need to be.

Like all institutions, policing wants to convince you that it is permanent, the only way forward, and in its best form now. But the truth is obvious.

In January 2015, Leon Kemp, Reggie Cunningham, Brittany Packnett, Johnetta Elzie, and I, a group who met during the protests and had since begun collaborating on solutions, realized that we were playing a game with only half of the pieces, a quarter of the board, and without knowing the rules, if there were any. In the days following the initial protests, we all heard more and more stories shared on the streets and through Twitter of black men, women, and children who were victims of police violence. It was becoming clearer that our collective demand that officers be indicted and hope that they were convicted was being roundly ignored. There was no accountability anywhere across the country, and we were trying to understand the how and why of it. Understanding the scope of what we were grappling with seemed like a necessary starting point.

What we quickly realized was that the federal government could tell you how many inches of rainfall there was in rural Missouri in the 1800s, but it could not provide reliable statistics on the number of people the police killed last year, let alone all the other forms of police violence impacting communities.

Around this time, Samuel Sinyangwe, a young policy expert and data scientist in San Francisco, reached out via Twitter with an interesting proposal. He'd been engaged in policy, and though he hadn't been with us in the streets in Ferguson, he knew that if the protests were ever to have substantive impact, we'd need data to inform a set of demands that had yet to emerge. He thought it would be possible to build the first comprehensive database and analysis of fatal police violence in the United States, including data on all types of violence that resulted in death. He wanted my help. A tweet turned into a phone call and then into Sam becoming part of our team.

The difficulty with building the database was that the police actively resist sharing this kind of information. If you get killed by a police officer in America, the only way that you currently appear in a data set is if a newspaper or other media outlet records your death. Any data that you can readily recount about police violence is the result of media outlet aggregation—there is no official government tally in which all police departments must participate. To this day, this reality has enabled politicians on both sides of the aisle to avoid addressing actual solutions while feeding the narrative that there is nothing that can be done besides offering platitudes. While the FBI technically collects data on killings by police through its annual Supplementary Homicide Report, this report is flawed in fundamental ways. For one, the data is self-reported; it relies on each of the nation's eighteen thousand police departments to submit data, which means that if a department doesn't report it, then there simply is no data at all. Florida, for instance, reported zero instances of police violence across the entire state between 2004 and 2014, which a simple Google search demonstrates is false.

As if that weren't problematic enough, the definition of police killing is so narrow that if it doesn't meet the bar of justifiable homicide, then it is grouped into regular homicide data. In practice, this means some of the homicides the federal government attributed to civilians were actually perpetrated by police. Even if the data was accurate, the way the government makes it accessible limits the type of analysis that can be done. It would be impossible to undertake analyses by place, race, and circumstance, as we ultimately did.

The Death in Custody Reporting Act of 2013 actually mandated the reporting of this data by police departments to the Department of Justice, and allowed the Department of Justice to cut 10 percent of funding to departments that did not comply. But reinforcing the complicity of the government in hiding the actions of the police from the public, this act has never been enforced and there remains no incentive for departments to provide accurate data.

MAPPING POLICE VIOLENCE (mappingpoliceviolence.org), as it was later named, sought to build on the work of Fatal Encounters and Killed by Police, the two major databases on police violence that attempted to do what the government could, but seemed not to want to, do. They pioneered a methodology for finding cases online without having to go through the police departments themselves. They set up elaborate ways of finding reports of police violence—compiling data from crowdsourced databases, local media reports, social media, and public records requests—and then logged them, which was especially important given that police departments are not required to publicly report instances of police violence.

Mapping Police Violence (MPV) merged these databases and then filled in missing information about race (40 percent of the data from those databases didn't include race), and added an armed/unarmed category. Our work involved analyses of the hundred largest cities in the country and visualized the data by race, city, and state in ways that had never been done before. MPV was the first comprehensive national analysis of fatal police violence in the United States, and it was in a format that made the information actionable. We had to do the work the government was unable or unwilling to do.

A few months following the release of Mapping Police Violence, the *Washington Post* and the *Guardian* released their own versions of the database. However, each had certain limitations: the *Washington Post*, for instance, only included instances of killings by officers who used guns, meaning that if an officer choked someone to death, that death would not be included; the *Guardian* omitted some off-duty killings. And each of those versions has data going back only as far as 2015, limiting the ability to identify trends and patterns over time.

In spite of the challenges, different methodological choices, and the likelihood that a small proportion of police violence incidents slip past media outlets, especially in smaller towns without newspapers or digital media, the overall findings were clear and compelling. We found that police kill twelve hundred people each year in America,* meaning one in every three people killed by a stranger in this country is killed by a

---

* Mapping Police Violence national database, https://mappingpoliceviolence .org.

police officer.* An additional fifty thousand people are hospitalized each year after being injured by police.† This violence disproportionately impacts black communities. Black people are three times more likely to be killed by police than their white counterparts and are more likely to be unarmed when killed.‡ Black people are more likely to be stopped, searched, arrested,§ and subjected to police use of force.⁵ Police violence is so prevalent in black communities that the majority of black youth have either personally experienced or witnessed police violence in their lives. And there was no accountability for this violence: in 97 percent of all police killings, the criminal justice system does not charge officers with any crime, and in 99 percent of cases the officer is not convicted.**

There were three even more striking things that we learned from the new analysis provided through MPV: The first is

---

* Patrick Ball. 2016. "Violence in the Blue." *Granta* 134: No Man's Land; The Online Edition (March 4, 2016), https://granta.com/violence-in-blue.

† Ted R. Miller et al., "Perils of Police Action: A Cautionary Tale from US Data Sets." *Injury Prevention*, published online first July 25, 2016. doi: 10.1136/injuryprev-2016-042023.

‡ Mapping Police Violence national database.

§ The Stanford Open Policing Project national database, https://openpolicing.stanford.edu/data.

⁵ Phillip Goff, PhD, Tracey Lloyd, PhD, Amanda Geller, PhD, Steven Raphael, PhD, and Jack Glaser, PhD. 2016. "The Science of Justice—Race, Arrests, and Police Use of Force." New York: Center for Policing Equity. http://policingequity.org/wp-content/uploads/2016/07/CPE_SoJ_Race-Arrests-UoF_2016-07-08-1130.pdf (accessed June 19, 2018).

** Mapping Police Violence national database.

that place matters—police violence varied by city in notable ways; second, police violence wasn't explained by crime rates as some had suggested; and last, police violence was more constant than we had previously understood.

In Baltimore, we found that every person killed by a police officer for as far back as our database went, to 2014, was a black man. In Cleveland, we showed that everyone killed since 2012, all ten people, were black, and seven were unarmed. We found that St. Louis has by far the highest rate of police violence in the country. Black men in St. Louis are killed by police at a rate twice as high as the US murder rate.

It made sense, then, that when we were in the streets during the protests, so many people had stories about a previous encounter that either they or a friend had had with the police. The St. Louis region was literally unlike any other when it came to the violence of the police.

We also found that in these hotspots of police violence nobody was focusing on it or intervening.* The Department of Justice was responding to where the most high-profile crisis was happening, largely as a result of unrest, but not always the places where police violence was most acute—like in Oklahoma City, where one in six homicides were committed by police; or Orlando and St. Louis City, which had the highest rates of police violence overall.

In each place where there was an uprising or a sustained

---

* Mapping Police Violence national database.

protest, there was a history of police violence beyond the sparking incident. In each case, we had the data to show a pattern of racism and police violence in that city to help people understand that this was a systemic problem, and that these were not isolated incidents.

Importantly, the data also provided us with the ability to confirm what we knew to be true anecdotally. We knew that the violence of the police was constant, but the data allowed us to tell the story of police violence in new ways. In 2015, for instance, there were only fourteen days where a police officer didn't kill someone. And of the sixty police departments in the top one hundred cities with available data, only the Riverside Police Department in Riverside, California, did not kill anyone in 2015.*

One of the analyses we did that still stuns me was to chart cities where only black people were killed by police. We already knew that police violence was disproportionately targeted to black people—black people are 41 percent of the victims despite being only 20 percent of the population in those sixty cities. But we also found out that fourteen police departments exclusively killed black people in 2015: Minneapolis, St. Louis, Baltimore, Atlanta, Kansas City (Missouri), Cleveland, Virginia Beach, Boston, Washington DC, Raleigh, Milwaukee, Detroit, Philadelphia, and Charlotte-Mecklenburg.†

As we reflected on the sustained, unchecked violence against black bodies at the hands of law enforcement, we

---

* Mapping Police Violence national database.
† Ibid.

realized just how intentional the control of this information was. In the absence of such information, police departments and their advocates were free to tell any story that served their interests. White America's deference to police served to shield it from interrogation, and the stories woven by the police only served to amplify their standing and delegitimize grievances.

Without data, it's hard to challenge the assumptions, stereotypes, and justifications that the police push. For instance, law enforcement commonly advances the notion that there is a relationship between community violence and police violence—that the police were more violent in communities that were themselves more violent, and that the police simply have to use more force in deadlier ways to maintain peace and order in dangerous cities. However, the data plainly does not support this: some police departments kill people far less frequently than others. The level of community violence in each city did not explain the level of police violence there.

Rather than being determined by crime rates, police violence reflects a lack of accountability in the culture, policies, and practices of the institutions of policing, as investigations into some of the most violent police departments in America have shown. We now had the data to help us understand the problem in a more holistic sense. Perhaps more important, the data illustrated the problem and gave people a different language to describe the realities communities had experienced.

The data also pointed to solutions. Why *were* police in some cities much less likely to kill people than others? What was it about the way a police department functioned that could explain their rate of violence? We were essentially operating from square one, since nobody had collected the data to even begin to draw data-driven conclusions about this issue. Not the academics and criminologists. Not the department of justice. Certainly not the police.

The secrecy of police departments extends beyond the numbers to the very policies themselves that outline when an officer is allowed to use deadly force. These "use of force" policies are almost never accessible, never publicly discussed. We were able to find them through a series of exhaustive Freedom of Information requests. We found each police department had different rules and standards of conduct, each a different system of accountability—or seemingly no system of accountability at all. Some departments had policies that required police to use tactics like de-escalation as a way to prevent police shootings. Others explicitly advised police that they did not need to use these tactics.

For example, we found that the San Francisco police have one of the most restrictive use of force policies in the nation.* Officers are required to de-escalate situations whenever possible. If that fails, they must exhaust all other reasonable means of addressing a situation using less lethal force before using their guns. And if those options all fail, officers are required to give a

---

* The Police Use of Force Project national database. The Police Use of Force Project. http://useofforceproject.org/ (accessed June 19, 2018).

verbal warning before using their guns. They are further required to report every time they point their guns at someone, and are restricted from using their guns against anyone who poses a threat only to themselves or who is inside a vehicle. Furthermore, each bullet an officer fires is evaluated on this standard—even if the first bullet fired is deemed justified, officers can still be held accountable for the circumstances in which they fired the next bullet during that encounter. Police in nearby San Jose, by contrast, don't follow these standards. The San Jose Police Department's use of force policy instructs officers that they "need not retreat or desist in the reasonable use of force. . . . There is no requirement that officers use a lesser intrusive force option before progressing to a more intrusive one."*

And it turns out these policies matter, a lot. Departments that had the most restrictive use of force policies were 72 percent less likely to kill people than those with the least restrictive policies.

When the protests began, I would have said, as many others have said, that police violence was bad people making bad decisions in the midst of a bad system. But now I realize that there are literally structures and systems that protect the police from accountability and encourage the types of behaviors and attitudes that do harm to communities.

---

* *Duty Manual* version 1. California: San Jose Police Department, February 23, 2015. https://static1.squarespace.com/static/56996151cbced68b170389f4/t/569a c02a1a520349a5086cdf/1452982356009/San+Jose+Use+of+Force+Policy.pdf.

When challenged, the police use the immense platform that society has afforded them to construct "truths" that are not based in fact. As people challenge the police to address statistics showing black people are more likely to be impacted by various forms of police violence, the police use their platform to blame black communities instead: *We just respond to the issues. We just go where the crime is,* they'll say as they rattle off statistics about crime in black communities. The police have harped on this line of thinking so relentlessly that now most everyone in America has heard it.

But the data shows this isn't true.

An analysis of marijuana arrests in New York City found that even when two areas call the police about marijuana at the same rates, police were more likely to arrest people in the area that has more black and brown residents. These disparities could not be explained by crime rates or rates of calling the police.*

It's a similar story for police killings. The police would have us believe that every officer who kills someone is in a dangerous situation, encountering a dangerous person, fearing for their lives, and thus forced to use deadly force to defend themselves or others from harm. We've all heard this narrative; the police have made it ubiquitous. But it too is a myth. We looked at the data on killings by police and found that

---

* Benjamin Mueller, Robert Gebeloff, and Sahil Chinoy. "Surest Way to Face Marijuana Charges in New York: Be Black or Hispanic." *New York Times*, May 13, 2018. https://mobile.nytimes.com/2018/05/13/nyregion/marijuana-arrests -nyc-race.html.

police are not only killing people in areas with higher crime rates, but also in areas with lower crime rates. Most police killings began with police responding to suspected nonviolent offenses or cases where no crime had been reported. And at least 57 percent of all cases involved someone who was not threatening anyone with a gun—cases that, in virtually any other country, would have been resolved without the police killing them.* The data is clear that community violence doesn't explain rates of police violence. The police were choosing to be violent regardless.

When challenged with these facts, the police construct new narratives to justify their behavior. When we identified more restrictive use of force policies as a solution to police violence, and presented them to the police, the police responded by saying such policies would "handcuff" officers, preventing them from protecting themselves or others from harm. They didn't have any data to support their conclusions. But we did. It turns out that the police departments with the most restrictive use-of-force policies are also the safest for officers and have similar crime rates as other departments.

IF THE CONTROL of information is what has historically provided police departments with the ability to shape an uncontested narrative of crime, criminals, and appropriate response,

---

* Mapping Police Violence national database.

it is the police unions that have solidified, through contracts, a secondary "justice" system for police that shields them from accountability.

In my positions in human capital departments in school systems before the protests began, part of my work entailed managing and implementing the labor agreements and teachers' contracts between the school district and the labor unions. I had seen that these documents contained rules and policies that those who'd never read them simply didn't know existed, or didn't realize that the school district operated a certain way because of a seemingly small clause in a contract.

That made me think about police union contracts as a site to explore.

It turns out that cities and police unions had been negotiating, behind closed doors, policies that made it nearly impossible to hold officers accountable. If you submitted a complaint of police misconduct too many days after an incident or decided to submit anonymously, contracts in many cities mandated that the police toss it out. If the police take more than 180 days to investigate the complaint, in many cities they have to toss it out. If they find that the officer being investigated has an extensive record of previous misconduct, they can't use that as a factor in determining discipline. And forty-three of the eighty-one contracts we reviewed required the officers' records of misconduct to be periodically purged from the system.* For

---

* *Duty Manual* version 1, San Jose Police Department.

instance, twelve-year-old Tamir Rice was killed by the Cleveland Police Department in 2014. In Cleveland, disciplinary records of police officers are removed from an officer's file after two years and written reprimands are removed after six months. The clause in the Cleveland police union contract reads: "Verbal disciplinary warnings and disciplinary written reprimands shall be removed from a police officer's record after six months, but all other disciplinary actions or penalties will be removed after two years from the date the discipline was administered."* But, why? Why should these be removed from an officer's file? It means that when an incident occurs, there's literally no way of us knowing whether the officer has a pattern of engagement in certain parts of a city, with certain demographics of people, or of manifesting certain behaviors. These clauses are meant to obscure key information from the process of accountability.

But there are other things that we found that make even less sense. The police union contract in Portland, Oregon, includes a clause that reads: "If the City has reason to reprimand or discipline an officer, it shall be done in a manner that is least likely to embarrass the officer before other officers or the

---

* Collective Bargaining Agreement between the City of Cleveland and Cleveland Police Patrolmen's Association (C.P.P.A) Non-Civilian Personnel, Effective April 1, 2013 through March 31, 2016. http://www.city.cleveland.oh.us/sites/default/files/forms_publications/2013-2016%20CPPA%20Non%20Civilian%20CBA.pdf?id=8302.

public."* How that plays out in practice is immensely unclear. But what is clear is that the police benefit from a set of structural protections unavailable to any private citizen.

It went deeper still. Even in cases where an officer does get disciplined for misconduct, most police union contracts give them an easy way out. Police union contracts in 73 percent of cities give officers who've been disciplined the ability to appeal to an arbitrator who can reverse the decision. In most of these cities, either the police officer being investigated or the police union, or both, help select the arbitrator who hears their case.† And so, according to the *Washington Post*, in places like San Antonio and Philadelphia, seven in ten officers who are fired for misconduct end up getting their jobs back (plus back pay) on appeal.‡

After focusing our analysis on the hundred largest cities, we are now working to analyze another eight hundred contracts, in cities with more than thirty thousand residents. Where union contracts fall off, too often the law itself is structured to

---

* Labor Agreement between the Portland Police Association and the City of Portland, July 1, 2013–June 30, 2017, Article 20.2. https://static1.squarespace.com/static/559fbf2be4b08ef197467542/t/55a26f71e4b0858890851ce6/1436708721758/Portland+police+contract.pdf.

† Stephen Rushin. Forthcoming 2018. "Police Disciplinary Appeals." *University of Pennsylvania Law Review* 167. https://thecrimereport.org/wp-content/uploads/2018/03/Rushin-Study.pdf.

‡ Kimbriell Kelly, Wesley Lowery, and Steven Rich. "Fired/Rehired." *Washington Post*, August 3, 2017. https://www.washingtonpost.com/graphics/2017/investigations/police-fired-rehired/?utm_term=.7e103cea5056.

protect the police in extraordinary ways. In California, for instance, the law states that if an investigation of an officer takes more than a year, then no discipline can be enacted on the officer, regardless of the outcome of the investigation. And who controls how long the investigations last? The police do, of course. And this matters because in 2015 the San Francisco police department sought to fire nine officers for exchanging racist text messages. But they appealed that decision on the basis that the investigation into their text messages took longer than a year. And the lower court eventually agreed with them and overturned their termination. This is because the law gives them a unilateral right to have an investigation completed at a speed that is not offered to another class of citizens. Luckily, a higher court disagreed with this interpretation, and this is now being litigated. But why should the police have such an extraordinarily different set of rules than everyone else?

In addition, most analyses and policy solutions regarding police violence focus primarily on men, given that 94 percent of the people killed by police are men. But this is relevant solely if we understand the entire scope of police violence to be actions that result in death. When we start to examine the police violence that doesn't necessarily result in death, like sexual harassment, sexual assault, and domestic violence, we gain a more expansive understanding of the problem *and* start to rightly identify the ways that women and members of the gay, trans, and queer communities are impacted by the violence of the police. As one can imagine, this data is even harder to find than information on those killed because in most cities and states, complaint data is not published or even collected in a way that makes it reportable.

And the laws in some places are working against us. In Louisiana, for instance, the so-called Officer's Bill of Rights states that any complaint of domestic violence is expunged from the officer's record if it's submitted anonymously, which it would likely be to avoid retaliation, and if it's not sustained by the department, which only one in thirteen complaints nationally are. In Baton Rouge, following the killing of Alton Sterling, Baton Rouge police chief Murphy Paul implored the public to "please stop resisting," and to always follow the orders of the police, and that if you think an officer has been biased, unprofessional, or acted unconstitutionally, to "pick up the phone and file a complaint."* He noted that when you do so, "most complaints will be resolved by the police department communicating or articulating to you that we had the legal right to do what we did."† Police Chief Paul is transparent in highlighting that filing a complaint will not likely lead to anything other than the police department reminding you that the rules are in their favor. It's also interesting that he asked the public to call to file a complaint, because in Baton Rouge it's impossible to call in a complaint of a police officer; they must be completed

---

* WDSU News. "Watch Again: BRPD Chief Gives New Info on Deadly Alton Sterling Shooting." Filmed [March 2018]. YouTube video, 19:48. Posted [March 2018].https://www.youtube.com/watch?v=BE3ylAnfmiI.
† Ibid.

either online or by mail, they cannot be anonymous, and they can be dismissed for a host of factors within ten days, at the discretion of Internal Affairs. This isn't accountability.

In 2017, 1,147 people were killed by the police, and officers were charged with a crime in only thirteen of these cases—1 percent of all killings by police. Nine of these thirteen cases had video evidence, most captured by police body and dash cameras.* We will continue to see video be important in bringing about any semblance of accountability in future cases. Body cameras, for instance, began being implemented before there were a clear set of best practices about their use. But now we know that police departments should not be able to upload the footage to third-party sites that use the video for surveillance or facial recognition technologies, the public and the district attorneys should have oversight of how the footage is used and accessed, officers should be prevented from reviewing the footage before completing initial reports, and citizens should be able to know if they have been filmed. Such footage can be an important tool in holding an officer accountable. In the absence of clear oversight, body cameras and other video-based tools can become avenues for surveillance of communities.

THE ADVERSE EFFECTS of irresponsible policing in communities are plain enough, and have become a popular topic;

---

* Mapping Police Violence national database.

but why, I wonder, don't more people challenge the institution of policing? I've now come to attribute the reasons to three things: the first is that people think that the absence of police being indicted, convicted, or fired for occurrences of police violence means that no wrongdoing took place, and therefore no changes are necessary; second, they believe that communities have so much conflict and that consequently policing is such a hard job that they accept instances of police violence as the cost of doing business; and last, people literally cannot imagine a way of managing conflict that is not rooted in negative power, the main style of policing.

In some ways it all makes sense. For so long the police controlled the narrative. They were the only ones who were regarded as telling the story from a position of credibility. But in this moment, their control over information is slipping, revealing an unchecked institution that is inherently incapable of policing itself and providing the set of services to the community that the community needs and desires.

As gut wrenching as it is to know the numbers, as infuriating as it is to read policies and contracts that enable brutality, I remain hopeful. I am hopeful because the choices that were made, the choices that resulted in our current state of affairs, are becoming clearer and clearer. The problem with the police isn't hidden. We can make a series of different choices. Will we?

FOUR

Bully and the Pulpit

The less you think about your oppression,
the more your tolerance for it grows.

—ASSATA SHAKUR

W hen I was nine years old, my babysitter put water on a grease fire and our house burned to the ground. My father, sister, and I moved to Grandma's house then, to a different part of town—leaving our small but separate bedrooms to now share a bed in her living room—about fifteen minutes away. And my sister and I started going to a new school. The thing that I remember most vividly from that year is the walk home from school. I remember the sweaty palms, the dry mouth, the bravado, the focus, the running. I remember Uncle Barry sometimes meeting us at the top of the hill.

And I remember the fear.

There was a bully on our block on the walk home, always present even when I couldn't see him. And every day, the ten minutes between the school parking lot and my grandmother's yard were full of anxiety. I've thought a lot about that year since then, especially after teaching sixth grade and seeing the way children are taught about power—about who has it and who doesn't; how to wield it and how to share it; and how one gains or loses it. And most important, what it is.

I've thought a lot more about the role of the bully too—about how he moves, adapts, and survives over time; about his source of legitimacy; about the impact of his power. Of late, I've thought about the bully in the context of our present world versus the world that we aim to create for the future, and considering him has transformed the way I think about both.

THE CURRENCY OF the bully is fear. It is what he trades in and what he feeds on—fear and confusion. He is violent in the obvious ways that we see and feel, in the physical assaults, but also in the quieter ways, the belittling and the taunts, the mental assaults. His goals are straightforward: to harm you and then convince you that no damage was done or that you deserved it. He aims to strip you of your power, to normalize the interaction so that you are simultaneously traumatized and left questioning if what you experienced actually happened, if what you felt was real.

Every day after school I anticipated him, even though he did not always show up in the ways I expected. But I was prepared, mentally and physically. I realize now that his power lay partly in his omnipresence—ever present in my mind even when he wasn't there in the flesh. And long after the bruises from the bully had healed, I was left living in a world where I expected violence, where the anticipation of trauma served as a survival mechanism. It was a world that looked subtly different from the one that I used to inhabit, a world without agency.

The bully aims to become the center of your everything. For me, the block was no longer the block where my grandmother lived, but the block with the bully. His trauma trapped me in the present where time, space, and my sense of self all folded in on themselves.

There were many days when I just wanted to get home. I didn't want to fight, I didn't want to run, I didn't want to find another way. I wanted to see my grandmother, my grandfather, my father. I wanted things to be normal. I now realize that the bully wants his tyranny to become the norm. And when he succeeds, he creates a burden that incessantly grinds on your spirit. It threatens your joy; it steals your innocence. The threat and the fear and the burden transform you. In the most literal sense, it changes the way that everyone in its orbit interacts with one another.

In the face of the bully, there are seemingly only two options: to challenge him or to accept him. I never understood the notion of "fight or flight" in this context, because "flight" would only be a temporary reprieve and not an actual stance.

I couldn't avoid the street forever, and I shouldn't have had to. "Fight" feels like an equally false option—overcoming the bully should not rest on adopting his tactics. When we accept these options, we run, we fight, we push back, because it seems like these are the only things we can do. In a world of incessant battles and their accompanying exhaustion, survival can become the overriding theme in how we think about living, and fear something that we unconsciously accept.

And sometimes, even as we challenge the bully, we come to accept him as just a part of our world.

Bullies don't just happen, they are enabled. There were bystanders who lived on my grandmother's block who chose to do nothing every single day. I think those people simply thought of bullying as another feature of childhood, a condition of growing up—just "kids being kids" or "boys being boys." They didn't suppose that simple child's play could have any lasting negative consequences, and thus did not consider themselves responsible for ending it. So they chose a third option that, in some ways, was the most dangerous: they chose to ignore him, to pretend that he and his tyranny were not what they were. And then there was the bully's family. They loved and cared for him but never corrected his behavior. Indeed, they never held a mirror up to show him what he was becoming.

When the world around you seems to accept bullying as normal, it's hard to imagine a world without it. And if the burden is inevitable, why fight against it?

————

I AM NO LONGER on the walk home, but I still know the bully.

We would recognize him today as much as Bull Connor and Jim Crow, the poll tax, police violence, the Black Codes, and redlining were recognized in their own time. The bully is the ideology of white supremacy. It is the notion that the lives of white people are inherently worth more than those of anyone else.

In many ways, we live in one of the bully's golden ages, a time when the mere mention of white supremacy is an anachronism. Absent the hoods and burning crosses, we presume the bully dead. But he's still operating in the shadows; he's just working through insidious means. The fact that many people refuse to acknowledge him means that we cannot dismantle what he has wrought. And in our blindness we've created a host of studies to explain away his legacy. In the meantime, he is at work. When we see 21 percent of kids of color in poverty, that is white supremacy at work. When we see a president refusing to allow immigrants from majority people-of-color countries into this country, that is white supremacy at work. Defunding public education, gerrymandering, and scaling back the Voting Rights Act are all manifestations of this ideology.

While we are able to share the pain that we experience, to organize, and to act in ways and with speed not heretofore possible, many of the tools that we now have at our disposal have simultaneously been turned against us. The platform that facilitated community building in Ferguson and beyond is now the preferred venue for our president to lie and mislead the public. We now know that our election was manipulated through the abuse of social media information on Facebook and the like. So though the tactics of the bully are tried and true, there is an unprecedented sophistication to the bullies of our time.

I KNOW THE WORLD better since that year that I lived at my grandmother's house. I know that there's no avoiding the bully—not when you move off that street, or exit that grade, or graduate from that school. In truth, the bully only becomes more vicious, more insidious, more institutionalized as time passes.

Paradoxically, many white people have been the collateral damage of policies enacted to uphold white supremacy. And thus we are all of us at risk. It's the trick of the bully that some of us may not realize the risk. Indeed, there are those who don't realize that the bully is coming for them too; they have not yet learned the fear. But white supremacy is about the fleecing of power to gain more power. So while the bully may not be after you today, he will surely target your car or hop over your fence in due time—because the bully is aiming to amass power, regardless of its victims.

In the face of this ever-present threat, silence is tempting.

Indeed, responding can be tiring and it may even seem futile in the midst of the onslaught. You just want the pain to end. Or to acknowledge the risk and walk confidently down the street despite it. While understandable, silence too easily becomes acceptance. But neither offers us a path to address the bully. The bully will take your lunch money, then tell you to go buy lunch; steal your car, then give you a driver's license. The bully likes to perform innocence when confronted, suggesting that we can all just move on, but we know this is one of his tricks.

To acknowledge the existence of the bully and his accompanying risks is not the same as accepting him as a permanent feature of our world. I know that if we accept trauma and fear, it wins.

Bullies don't just go away. Their legacies don't just disappear. The bully must be confronted intentionally, his impact named and addressed. Even so, it seems there's no clear consensus on how to deal with the bully on our blocks. Do we confront him? Match violence with violence? Do we ignore him, or try to kill him with kindness? I don't think there's a silver bullet to handling the bully, no one-size-fits-all strategy. But the right strategy has to be rooted in a context bigger than the immediate one, has to be rooted in more than aiming to end the presence of the bully himself. We must focus on the type of world we want to live in and devise a plan for getting *there,* as opposed to devising a strategy centered on opposition.

Still, there may yet be a general blueprint for beating the

bully. He is effective on the street because he knows the street. He knows which neighbors turn a blind eye. He knows what sections of the street have the lowest traffic and are farthest from the objecting gaze of concerned neighbors. The bully picks his spots. So we need to identify and name the things that enable him, in order to address them head-on and remove them from the playing field. Then we need to expose the bully and all the ways he is able to perpetrate his actions, stripping him of the agency that he seeks to strip from us.

We need to remind the peers of the bully that they benefit from bullying even if they are not themselves the transgressors. Indeed, they benefit from it, but they are tarnished by it. To chip away at the humanity of select groups is to chip away at humanity itself.

As long as the trauma, the pain he causes, is present, the work of exposing the bully will be present. We identify what props him up and we remove it: If he is propped up by the death of a people, then empowering and rescuing become part of that exposure. If he is propped up by artificial division or the propagation of false information, then partnering together and focusing on truth are part of that exposure. If he is propped up by his effort to pull us apart, to widen the gap between winners and losers, then standing in solidarity with the disenfranchised and oppressed becomes part of that exposure. If he is propped up by a shift in the focus of the work, then reminding ourselves of our main objectives becomes part of that exposure.

When we think about engaging and defeating the bully, we must remember that it isn't just about getting home, it's about thriving, and that our goal is not to switch places with the bully, but to end bullying.

This is by no means an easy task. The presence of the bully is difficult to overcome and the residue is difficult to shake. I stress the importance of imagining our ideal world because we naturally gravitate toward methods for achieving our desired outcomes. Indeed, we focus on tactics—how do we beat the bully?—but we don't always remember to prepare for the day when the bully is no more. We will need a vision for that time too. If we don't have a vision for our desired future, how can we plan to achieve it? If you cannot imagine it, you cannot fight for it. When we confront the bully, we are confronting our fear and reclaiming our imagination. There are those who cannot imagine a block without a bully. We must all imagine the block without a bully, otherwise we cannot get there.

When I am most in fear of succumbing to the bully, of allowing him to redefine my space, my world, I am reminded that the street existed before the bully did. We were free before we were enslaved. We are born to love before we know pain.

When I was nine, I didn't know how to challenge the bully. I thought I was alone. The task of conquering my fear, of exposing him, loomed so large in my mind's eye that I was overcome by it. If I hadn't gone to Ferguson and stood toe to toe with other protesters on the streets calling for justice, naming our bully, and saying enough is enough, I'm not sure I'd have the courage to confront him today.

In each generation there is a moment when young and old, inspired or disillusioned, come together around a shared hope, imagine the world as it can be, and have the opportunity to bring that world into existence. Our moment is now.

FIVE

The Choreography of Whiteness

The world does not need white people to civilize others. The real White People's Burden is to civilize ourselves.

—ROBERT JENSEN

I had to learn that white people could be wrong.

In the summer months leading up to sixth grade, we made our way back to the old burnt-down house. But we weren't to be there for long; my father had other plans. For the better part of a year, he'd been picking up extra shifts stocking shelves at a local corner store called Rudy's. He'd been working and saving with the hopes of giving us the life that he never had. And before long, we were packing up and moving on. The new house was in Catonsville, one block over from the Baltimore City line, on a street called Delrey Avenue. Though my father's name is Calvin, he's gone by Ray his entire life. My sister, TeRay, and I were much less enthusiastic about living on a street called Delrey—especially me—but our father took the likeness as an affirmation. And thus Ray, TeRay, and DeRay would live on Delrey.

We split our life between weekends at my grandmother's house in a predominantly black part of the city, and school days in the county, where our community was almost entirely white. That school was the first place I'd ever consistently been in a setting with white people. I'll never forget the first time I saw white parents walk into school demanding that classes and schedules be changed for their children. Or when they challenged the teachers on their children's grades and chose entire course trajectories for them, insisting on AP and honors classes, and requesting unit plans. I never saw that at my old schools. It wasn't that those parents didn't care about their children, but rather that they didn't expect to be able to make demands on how the academic program was configured.

I couldn't imagine my father doing that. He graduated from high school and did not attend college, and to him attending school was a privilege and teachers were sacred. My father did not conceive of the school system as something to be navigated, as it was for the white parents, but instead considered it a gift that we should have been grateful to participate in. As a single father, he was trying to make a way for us that he had only previously dreamt of. I mean, he saved and borrowed so that we could go to schools that he thought would put us on a better educational trajectory. Before I saw him do it, I never knew that people actually made decisions about buying homes because of the local schools. I thought that was just something I saw on TV. But he held education in the highest regard, to the point of actually being deferential to the school staff. I remember one day he told me that he would always believe the teacher if they called to report me for misbehaving. "But what if they hit me?" I asked. He replied something along the lines of, "I hope that doesn't happen, because I'm going to believe them." I think there was only a bit of a joke in that. He simply hadn't been raised to challenge authority.

I'll never forget the day one of my teachers said something that was wrong—she made a mistake—and it was the first time I had ever seen a white person be wrong. I don't even remember the details of her mistake, but I remember realizing that she was wrong, and I can still see her correcting herself. It's weird to say it now, but as a kid I didn't know that white people could be wrong. I certainly hadn't seen a wrong white person on TV.

I grew up watching whiteness work, watching it dance and adapt itself around me, demanding that I dance and adapt to it, shaping how the world sees it and therefore how people make decisions and think about possibilities.

I understood whiteness before I had the language to describe it.

I had to learn the difference between whiteness and white people, and how to talk about that difference. The former, an enforced power dynamic that confers power exclusively on white people, is sustained by building and manipulating systems and structures. This dynamic situates white people as normal and nonwhite people or people of color as a deviation from the norm. White people are both the primary beneficiaries *and* the carriers of whiteness, regardless of any individual person's intent. The distinction between whiteness and white people is important, because whiteness is an idea made flesh, an idea that has become so potent and ingrained that, to some, uprooting it seems almost impossible. But it is an idea nonetheless, and one that has changed over time. To be white, or considered white, is really just another way of saying who can leverage the power of whiteness without repercussion. And whiteness is rooted in domination.

If whiteness is considered the standard, it is also believed to be primordial. Indeed, to some, it is organic, pure, and uncorrupted, and thus superior. Notably, it is this belief that created the other contours of race, that made race become a game of winners and losers, of haves and have-nots. It made flesh carry an idea of worthiness, of deservedness, of value. Racism, then, is rooted in whiteness.

And racism manifests in two ways: through white supremacy, and through antiblackness.

White supremacy is the belief that white people are superior to people of color, and it is perpetuated not simply by individual beliefs but by institutions that codify and thus reinforce it. Conversely, antiblackness is the set of beliefs, practices, and actions that harm, discard, or exploit people of color, with especial severity for black people. The distinction is significant, because white people are traditionally the only white supremacists, but other people of color can participate in anti-blackness. The Ku Klux Klan and the alt-right are prime examples of white supremacy as they clearly express a belief in "white nationalism" and a "white state." Both are possible only with the subjugation of nonwhite folks. On the flip side, colorism, the preference among people of color toward lighter skin over darker skin, is an example of antiblackness. It is possible for people to think of blackness as wholly negative and not simultaneously think that whiteness is superior, though antiblackness is heavily influenced by the ideology that white supremacy has created.

WHAT DOES IT MEAN that whiteness is an idea and a set of values and not a natural law, as some would like to believe? Indeed, that it is an idea with consequences? We talk about whiteness as an idea with consequences so that we can see how the idea itself leads to actions, and then we can develop a plan for mitigating those actions. Because white is defined as normal or standard, the people who benefit from it (i.e., white people) often struggle to see it operating, because to them it is simply the natural order of the world. Whiteness is seemingly so ubiquitous that it appears to be invisible. This is why understanding white privilege is important. It is the act of seeing the seemingly invisible.

It is the work of white people to undo whiteness. As the writer Michael Harriot has noted, "White people who are quiet about racism might not plant the seed, but their silence is sunlight."* I do not say this to suggest that people of color have no role; we do. But we will never undo an idea so insidious alone. It begins with white people unpacking and acknowledging that the system is designed for and benefits them in ways that are solely based on their whiteness and not on any attribute that they possess as individuals—this is what we call white privilege.

Whiteness is not a hardwired, immutable, intractable part of the world we live in, even if or when it feels like it is. I grew up explaining it, responding to it, and believing in its myths. I had to learn to believe in something else. Learning that white people could be wrong was just the beginning for me, the beginning of seeing a world beyond whiteness as standard. It is a different type of work to survive whiteness, to grow up in its context, and to learn to make meaning independent of it. To challenge it, to escape its grasp, and to love oneself in spite of it—this is the work of people of color.

To understand how whiteness works across generations, imagine buying the winning lottery ticket for the largest lottery in history, and then having someone steal your ticket. You try to get it back, but you fail. The thief then cashes in, and his family benefits from this wealth for the next twenty generations. Later, your kids are able to identify that the theft happened. But when they ask for recompense, they are told that nothing can be done,

---

* Michael Harriot. "White People Are Cowards." *The Root*, June 19, 2018, https://www.theroot.com/white-people-are-cowards-1826958780.

that the past is the past, and that they need to move on. But what does moving on look like? How does one move on when the original harm isn't addressed and when the consequences of that harm continue to cause suffering?

This is how whiteness works. White people benefit from a set of choices in the past that still have an impact today, and though almost no one now living has caused the initial harm, they benefit. To recognize the original harm is not the same as repairing it, though repair is, of course, impossible without recognition. The point is that active theft isn't required for people to participate in and perpetuate the harm.

Another example to consider could take place in a middle-school classroom. A teacher tells her students that they need to bring in their own rulers to use on an upcoming test. So the kids go home and tell their parents they need rulers. Some parents go to the local store, we'll call it ABC Grocer, and buy the rulers. Others buy rulers elsewhere. Unbeknownst to the kids or their parents, the rulers that were shipped to ABC Grocer had a manufacturing defect. The kids who used those rulers generally performed worse on the test. When a student spots an error on her ruler, she brings it to the teacher's attention, but she's told, "That's unfortunate, but we've already moved on. You'll just need to make sure you have a properly functioning ruler next time." The child may go home to complain, but if her parents are anything like my father, the teacher would get deference.

Whiteness is the dynamic that creates a set of kids who performed better because they had the right ruler. Their superior performance then poises them for advanced classes the following year, setting them on an entirely different trajectory for life. Now on two different tracks, the self-worth and perceived ability of some will be inflated, and will necessarily be deflated for others. And kids on both sides will simply assume that this is the natural order of things, how the world is supposed to function. The kid with the bad ruler might never see someone overcome their disadvantage, so she just buckles down and does her best given the circumstances.

Now, years later the ruler manufacturer is discovered to have known about the defective rulers. Instead of throwing them out, it offered to sell them at a steep discount. Some store owners took advantage of their offer and bought them at the discounted price. The owner of ABC Grocer knew that his customers had less means, so he bought them and reduced the price, but still made a healthy profit. After all, he rationalized, how serious is a flawed ruler anyway?

It also turns out that upon becoming aware of the defective rulers, the parents who purchased them brought the problem to the attention of the school board. The parents of the kids who scored higher wanted to make sure their kids maintained class standing to get at the limited number of advanced spots the following year. These parents argued for fairness and equality *next year,* for standards that would affect future students. And, importantly, they argued that since their kids didn't *mean* to do anything wrong, they shouldn't be punished, even if that meant other kids were being punished. To them, they didn't cheat or exploit an unfair advantage. And in asking that the results remain, the parents were just fighting for their kids.

It's easy to read this story as one of poverty and access and not necessarily about race. To be sure, the allegory is imperfect. But when race is the axis by which poverty and access function, it simply can't be ignored. Moreover, many things happen at the intersection of race and class, but race has a way of tipping the scales in a negative way even for people of means.

This is whiteness. Some know about the advantage; some don't. And though not every white person is a cheater, every white person still benefits from what happened, and that's the point.

Even when the cheating is exposed, it doesn't change the impact of what has already taken place.

And the farther you move from the initial incident, fewer people believe that it happened at all, and that the source of the ultimate outcome was intentional. As time goes by, it's increasingly hard to trace the event's impact. We think, How could someone allow this incident to become so bad? Or, How do we fix it, it happened so long ago? Those who advocate for some sort of fix or acknowledgment of the problem become the people who "refuse to move on."

Whiteness is an ideology that says that some people will always have more than others. Predicated on theft and exploitation, it actively profits off the prejudices, systems, and institutions that promote inequality. If whiteness were a business, we could think of white people as the founders. At first the company was private. Over time, they sold pieces of ownership to other groups. To become eligible for a stake, you not only needed the resources but also had to meet certain membership requirements. With each sale, the existing members profited, with the founders profiting the most. The criteria that makes someone eligible to buy shares has shifted over time, and the cost of a share has increased significantly. The power of whiteness lies in its ability to make people conform to its membership requirements. And because the benefits of membership pass on from generation to generation, a legacy member can take for granted, or become blind to, the benefits. When people "unpack their privilege," they are owning the benefits afforded their membership.

But too often, in practice, rather than serving as a catalyst for tackling whiteness, this unpacking serves as an end point in itself. For people in a position of privilege this work is certainly necessary, but it alone is not sufficient, as it only examines an individual's relationship to whiteness. If we are ever to change the system, we will need to use the individual's relationship to whiteness as a lens to see how the decisions aggregated over time intentionally created these disparities.

When James Baldwin says that white is a metaphor for power, he is actually noting that whiteness is a metaphor for *power over* as opposed to *power with*—that it is automatically imbued with a sense of domination. He is reminding us that our goal as people of color is never to become white; that is, it is never to extend the idea of domination, but rather to change the conception of power itself. Indeed, we must end the idea of domination as an organizing principle in society. Audre Lorde said it best when she spoke of fighting old power on its own terms: "We cannot fight old power in old power terms only. The only way we can do it is by creating another whole structure that touches every aspect of our existence, at the same time as we are resisting."*

It's common to hear well-meaning white people come to their own defense over the legacy of power and privilege that they've inherited. Individual arguments tend to fall into one of several categories: guilt, shame, denial, mockery, or indifference. From institutions, the response is either denial or justification of entitlement.

Guilt is manifested when people feel that they have taken racist actions in the past and feel bad about having taken those actions. Guilt, as Brené Brown notes, does motivate people to change their actions, but it is not a sustainable motivator. This sounds like, "I now understand what I did wrong or the things that were problematic in the past, and I will change moving forward." The difficult part of white guilt for white people is that it forces them to reckon with their past. It often pushes people to focus so much on personal transformation, however, that they forget that there is a larger system that led to their

---

* Audre Lord, *Sister Outsider: Essays and Speeches*. New York: Crossroads Press, 2007.

personal advantages. To get through guilt, it's important to remain focused on the fact that although the past is fixed, the present and future are very much in play. Atoning for the past is not just an inward act but a forward-looking proposition, one that should be predicated on actions and decisions that actively dismantle guilt through real-time change.

Shame is manifested when people feel that they are themselves bad and/or racist, not that the actions they have taken are bad and/or racist. This is a fixed way of thinking about one's identity. Such people often feel that because whiteness is rooted in exploitation, and because they cannot be unwhite, that they are inherently bad. To deal with this shame, white people will sometimes acknowledge the underlying injustice, but create an exception that says: *I didn't participate in it.* It often is verbalized as, "But I didn't do it. I didn't do anything. I'm a good person." Or, "I worked hard for everything I have. Whiteness didn't help me. I don't even know what whiteness is." Or, "White pain is pain too," as if there is a parallel between individual trauma and systemic trauma. The way that white people can or should work through shame is to remember that while they have all made decisions, they are not their past decisions. Shame destroys us and forces us to double down on our beliefs. But if white people understand that they are not the decisions they've made, they can begin to see a pathway to change.

Denial is related in many ways to shame, but instead of distancing themselves from the problem, denial refutes the existence of the problem. It says that white supremacy and racism are not real, and that claims of either are overblown. Denial is also manifested as the performance of innocence, the perplexity in the statement, "I simply don't know what you're talking about." I gave a talk recently where a student challenged me by asking, "Why are you making everything about race? How do you know that redlining was racist?" The same sentiment has been expressed to me in statements like, "You don't know how it was; you weren't there." I've found that those employing the tactic of denial will often bombard me with questions—regardless of whether the questions bear any relevance to the matter at hand—with the express purpose of pushing the conversation to a completely new space.

When the student started to ask me about how I knew that redlining was racist, I told him about the literal red lines drawn on maps by the Federal Housing Administration, and then I asked him, "When I show you the maps and show you that red lines were specifically in black communities and not others, will you still deny it?" He then shifted his stance to suggest that whatever the nature of the design—racist or not—redlining did not have the impact that I was claiming it had. That I'd answered his original criticism was suddenly beside the point.

I've found that in order to respond to those engaged in denial, we must shift the cognitive burden to them. We do this by building a chain of questions that force them to reinvestigate basic truths, which then lead to larger acknowledgments.

But for some, this tactic only results in distraction, as there is no earnest engagement that will shift them, because they know that they are engaging in lies.

Mockery presents itself when people blame the oppressed, as if it is their collective choice to be so. This underlying attitude restricts the generosity of spirit afforded to disadvantaged groups. Instead of acknowledging that poverty might be experienced differently and more fully by people who had been systematically denied access to the building blocks of wealth and industry for the majority of America's existence, the focus is on adding work requirements to food stamps and housing. The imposition of work requirements is used as a bulwark to prevent the poor from exploiting poverty for a "free ride," or to incentivize them to get away from the poverty line, as if hovering just above or below the line is something to aspire to. There is a pervasive focus on making those who have suffered from whiteness both prove their oppression and defend the interventions aimed at addressing the effects of that oppression. The familiar earn-deserve paradigm rears its ugly head. And it sounds like, "Well, if they had made different choices then they'd be able to buy a house." Or when low standardized-test scores for third-graders signal, "Something simply must be *wrong* with the kids," the notion is perpetuated that the oppressed are to blame, and not the system.

There is also indifference. People who are so removed from the oppressed that oppression simply plays out at the periphery of their lives, if it all. They are aware of injustice and hardship, but it's not present enough to evoke a response like the four cited above. Indifference is the absence of attention, the notion that an issue need not be discussed or attended to. The indifferent offer that the issues are so big that they aren't necessary to engage with, or are just a feature of the world—like starving children in African nations or ethnic cleansing in Syria. Their indifference can be a by-product of the communities in which they live or their lack of proximity to people of color or those who experience visible hardship. As income stratification continues to increase along socioeconomic lines, indifference is poised to become a more common characteristic of white people and those who benefit from whiteness.

Individuals have individual responses, but institutions are the collective response of individuals, hardened over time. Institutions have a set of behaviors that incubate in denial and are manifested in the behaviors of entitlement. When an institution attempts to wrestle with its role in perpetuating white supremacy or to recognize how whiteness has influenced its design and function, it can be unwilling to engage in a narrative that acknowledges the structural issues at play that promote oppression. It can, for example, say with a straight face that because we are fifty years removed from the poll tax, the need for a Voting Rights Act is moot. Here the institution focuses on the last fifty years of "fairness" under the law and ignores the preceding two-hundred-plus years of oppression that created the structural unfairness in the first place. Institutional denial reflects an unwillingness to acknowledge historical or active systems and structures that work to uphold racism. The manifestation of this denial is an entitlement that claims unearned benefits. It puts the onus on the oppressed to not only make the case for the impact of their exploitation, but also to manufacture the solutions. The ultimate portrayal of denial is a defensive stance that says that even though things were obtained by exploitative means, the recipients deserved them.

I OFTEN TWEET "watch whiteness work" to describe the way that whiteness is manifesting itself in a particular moment. Once, someone sent me a long email, frustrated with my use of the phrase. He was particularly upset that I did not say "white supremacy" or "racism." I didn't have time to email him a reply, but I did email him to ask for his number. I called him, and as we talked I tried to push him to understand the way that whiteness functions outside of examples like lynching and enslavement.

I reminded him that when we go to the store and buy "nude" clothing, it looks like his skin and not mine. And that Band-Aids are a skin tone—again, his and not mine. And that when we read books, the characters are white until named something else. I was explaining to him that all these things are about power, they're all a function of the fact that whiteness is normative, that whiteness has been set up as the standard and that everything else is a deviation from it. And that this is its own form of power and not a result of hard work or self-mastery.

There are other examples of whiteness at work that people are either unaware of or have roundly overlooked. In high school, I thought a map was a map. I'd never considered that the display of countries and continents was also a political act. It was much later that I would learn about the Mercator projection, the sixteenth-century map projection that displays the continent of Africa as similar in size to other countries when in fact it is much larger. In the *Economist,* they note the following about the projection: "Africa looks about the same size as Greenland under the Mercator projection, for example, even though it is in fact 14 sizes bigger." And the Mercator projection is the template for Google Maps, OpenStreetMap, and Bing.*

The same underlying principle is at work when people try to say that the Confederacy was not about white supremacy. All we have to do is look at the Cornerstone speech, delivered by Confederate vice president Alexander Stephens for insight into the founding principles of the confederacy:

> Our new government is founded upon exactly [this] idea; its foundations are laid, its cornerstone rests, upon the great truth that the negro is not equal to the

* Sophie Morlin-Yron. "What's the Real Size of Africa? How Western States Used Maps to Downplay Size of Continent." CNN, March 23, 2017. https://www.cnn.com/2016/08/18/africa/real-size-of-africa/index.html.

white man; that slavery subordination to the superior race is his natural and normal condition. This, our new government, is the first, in the history of the world, based upon this great physical, philosophical, and moral truth.

There is no way to support the Confederacy and not simultaneously support white supremacy.

THE IMPORTANCE OF defining whiteness lies in the fact that without doing so, a well-meaning white person cannot meaningfully engage in the work of breaking it down. But this is only the first step and it is important only insofar as a person who benefits from whiteness can take the personal experience and link it to the structural experience, and is able to identify and acknowledge an intentional set of structures, systems, and institutions that allow the privilege to manifest. If white people stop at self-exploration or unpacking their privilege, they easily fall into a cycle of self-congratulation in which they are celebrated for seeing what people of color around them have always had to see and live through, for survival. And this cycle of self-congratulation doesn't actually change anything about the power dynamic. But it does make white people feel better. Memorizing and reciting is not the same as learning. And it is only through learning that allies are poised to partner in the work.

It seems that "allyship" is the buzzword of the day, and we

need allies too. However, too many people claim to be "woke," but cannot see beyond their own experience. And, thus, I have grown tired of the notion of an ally. I prefer the language of an "accomplice." An ally loves you from a distance. An accomplice loves you up close. We need allies to make the transition to accomplices. An ally is someone who has unpacked her personal privilege but hasn't yet made the link to institutional issues and is not willing to risk anything besides her mental comfort. An accomplice rolls up her sleeves and engages in the work that is beyond her. She'll march in the streets, yes. But an accomplice also faces her own participation in whiteness, acknowledges it, and then looks beyond that personal acknowledgment to identify how her awareness can be applied to changing the systems and mind-sets that prop up the system.

The myth of meritocracy, this notion that hard work is rewarded and that anyone can rise above their circumstances, is pernicious because it's based on the idea that the true influence of one's trajectory is one's personal ability and motivation. But we know that this is not true, especially when race is involved. We know that the average white high school graduate earns more than the black college graduate, for instance. We also know that marginalized youth who grow up believing that their hard work is a determinant of their social outcome actually experience a decrease in self-esteem and have an increased engagement in risky behavior—because meritocracy isn't real. Even the best policies struggle to have the desired impact with regard to shifting racial disparities, because racism remains so potent.

Some have said that whiteness traffics in distraction, and I think this may be true. But the distraction is in deception, in pushing you to ignore whiteness's investments in itself and to never ask whiteness to do for others what it has done for white people. It is no surprise that the solutions that are suggested for people of color always require people of color to be exceptional—they must be some combination of small-business owners, college graduates, highly motivated, etc. They aren't simply worthy because they are human, because they are alive. So when we talk about things like closing the racial wealth gap and mention that we could give people of color low-interest housing loans like we did exclusively for white people in the past, the response is that this simply isn't a viable option. Or that we should focus exclusively on small businesses, as if the only people who deserve not to live in abject poverty are people who want to be small-business owners. But white people who were regular, unmotivated, but just white benefited from the GI Bill, from redlining, and from so many other programs and services.

Whiteness is an idea and a choice. We can choose differently. We can introduce new ideas to replace it. We have the tools to build something altogether anew.

SIX

I Was Raised
By Magic

*Doubt is not a denial but an integral
part of faith. . . . But doubt does not
have the final word. The final word
is faith giving rise to hope.*

—JAMES H. CONE

*I prayed for twenty years but received no
answer until I prayed with my legs.*

—FREDERICK DOUGLASS

I t wasn't that I didn't believe in God, but that I believed in Storm more. The X-Men seemed somewhat more relatable to me than a Jesus who died for my sins and rose again. I understood what it was like to be different, to be seen as a mutant of sorts, more than I understood what it was like to be the blond, blue-eyed man on a crucifix I had seen Jesus depicted as.

I went to church because I had to. Church was about more than God to me then. Or rather, it was not about God so much as it was about the other things. It was the cadence, the rhythm of blackness in one room, all of us focusing on something other than our pain for this one moment, asking for relief from a power greater than our own, able to cry and dance and sing and laugh and feel free. It was this feeling of freedom that I most remember from church, that it taught me. That there could be moments in this world when black people could come together and feel an unguarded joy, when we could be given and we could share a happiness that may, at its best, take us through the week until we needed the next dose next Sunday.

But for my father, church was holy. He often credits his recovery from drug addiction as being possible only because of his relationship with God, a power greater than himself. He even thought he might have been called to be a preacher. One of the memories that I'll never forget is watching him preach about Jesus's crown of thorns on the cross. But for me, church was a place I went because I had to go.

I did not truly know God then. I said my prayers when I ate because it was a ritual. And I participated in singing the music because it was beautiful, and because of the way the rhythm moved not only through our bodies but through the air. It was its own marvel, its own force field.

I knew Storm. I knew everything about her that I could know from the cartoons, which was admittedly less than I would've known had I been into comic books as a child. I knew she was a goddess. I knew how she led the X-Men while letting them lead. I knew how she had the power to control the elements but never let that power drown out the power of her peers.

I knew women who reminded me of Storm—women like

my great-grandmother, and my sister, and Robin, my first boss when I was a teenage youth organizer with Baltimore's Safe and Sound Campaign, who has always been like another mother to me.

Storm taught me how to imagine. But she wasn't the only one. Professor X did too. And so did Rogue. I learned how to believe in things that seemed impossible, how teams worked, how decisions were made, and that magic was not only possible but real. I learned how to live beyond the constraints—just like they did. Gravity? It didn't matter anymore. Rain? Storm could control it. Wind? She had that too. Snow? Storm, again, in control.

For some people, their sense of possibility comes from their understanding of faith, the idea of salvation being a guidepost offering a glimpse into a life beyond the life of now. But that never made sense to me. Storm did.

So much of what trauma does to us is trap us in the present; it traps us in its constraints. We often see the limitations all around us because we need to see them in order to survive. Not to see them would be deadly. We become gifted at knowing how far to push before the world pushes back on us. But Storm? Storm didn't live in a world with those constraints. And for thirty minutes each weekend, neither did I.

Our superheroes are more than just entertainment. I can't help but think that in a world with as much chaos as ours, the prominence of Iron Man, Wonder Woman, and Black Panther is no coincidence. I even think about the games we played, games like Mario Kart. I was often frustrated at how the power-ups were distributed in that game, that the closer you got to the number-one position, the weaker the power-ups you got. But now it makes sense. The people who are further behind should get more power-ups, more support, to help them along the way. The superheroes and these games were teaching us so much.

While I don't have the time to watch Storm every weekend anymore, I still carry the lessons she taught me—about leadership, about friendship, about power, and about right and wrong. And I still carry their world, a world much bigger than any world I've ever known, in me.

I now realize that I learned how to imagine because of those cartoons and games. Before the fire and our move to the county, we lived in a row house tucked away in West Baltimore. We went outside in the front and back yards, which were tiny, and we walked to school every day. But when we went to my grandmother's house in another tucked-away neighborhood, the yard was massive. As a kid, it felt as big as a football field—we could play all types of games like baseball, kickball, hide-and-seek; we could have cookouts and parties. It was much larger than our yard, which was about as big as our front porch, and it felt like another opening in the world, a portal to something beyond what I thought was possible. And there were other things beyond that yard that were opening the world for me.

I got a computer, a laptop, when I was eleven. It was the

only thing that I wanted for Christmas, and I've had a computer ever since. Even with the access that the internet provided, my world was still small—I knew the things in front of me best and had not imagined that life could be different for me, even as I saw on TV and on the internet how it was different for other people. Everything still felt so distant, like those things were meant for others to experience and for me to simply watch.

WE LEARN THE constraints that we face intimately, mostly as a matter of survival. I knew how far to press for a new toy, because I had seen the pain in my father's face enough times in the past when he said that he couldn't afford them. I knew to accept that we would always get my sister's favorite cereal at the grocery store, because we could only afford one box. I knew how proud my father was when we went "school shopping" during the summer and how those clothes needed to last until the winter. And I knew how big a deal it was that I finally got a pair of glasses at LensCrafters, and that if they ever broke, I just might not be able to see again.

We learn the fabric of our constraints early. They become a part of the way we move through the world, a part of the way the world moves around us. But sometimes, our world becomes those constraints. They become our road map and our guide, ushering us from one goalpost to another.

X-Men was all about constraints too. On every episode,

they faced a challenge that was bigger than themselves, even with their superpowers. But a part of each mission was to think of another angle, another way of defeating the bad guy in the midst of seemingly overwhelming odds. They never saw the challenge in front of them as fixed and permanent, but always as malleable and the result of choices.

I recently phoned an expert on public housing because I was fascinated with how long waiting lists are for housing in cities across the country—sometimes as many as thousands of names—and I wanted to understand why. "So if I gave you a billion dollars for X city, and I told you that you needed to figure out a way to alleviate the public housing list without re-creating the projects," I offered, "how would you do it?" She paused. And then the first four sentences she uttered were all about the constraints. She explained that there is not enough land; that housing projects might need to be a solution; that it might be hard to identify everyone; that we've never seen a list be cleared in an equitable way quickly. I left that call reminded that there is an industry that exists to identify the constraints, and then there are a smaller set of people who understand constraints as the result of choices and not as permanent fixtures. And this smaller set of people generally tends to have less influence than they should.

Consider the issue of mass incarceration. I think that three things will always remain true: first, there will always be rules; second, there will always be people who break the rules; and last, there will always need to be some form of consequences.

And when I say rules here, I mean standards that communities set as norms. And when I say consequences, I mean a structured or standardized response to the breaking of said rules.

Now, everything else is open to change. We *should* have more public conversations about how to enforce the rules. To be sure, some people may need to be separated from society as a consequence of their behavior, but if rehabilitation is the goal of any period of separation, then it should not look like solitary confinement. Indeed, no one should be locked in a small room for days, months, and years as a means of behavioral adjustment.

I'm not convinced that the people who search for kids who skip school should be the same people who try to solve murders. What if instead of calling the police to report kids hanging around outside, people called after-school providers or community-center staff and asked if there were ways to engage those kids?

What if every kid was provided with a set of library books from birth to senior year in high school?

If faith is our belief that our world *will* be better, and hope our belief that it *can* be better, imagination is what allows us to navigate between the two, to paint a picture of the future that we can one day touch, feel, bring into being. Both require a relationship with the future that is not solely dependent on the past. Both require a belief in things yet to come.

We can't fight for what we can't imagine. So much of the work of bringing about a better world will be rooted in us seeing that something else is possible. It is easier to see and understand a world that has already existed. Part of the allure of the "Make America Great Again" slogan is that the imagery and mental model already exist. Those who tout this mantra are asking us to engage in recall, and they are using images of the past to push us there. We have lived in a time before when white supremacy, bigotry, and hatred were firmly entrenched in our laws and practices. We do not need to imagine that time; it is etched in our memories and our bodies.

When we talk about freedom, however, we are forced to imagine it, because we have not yet lived in a time where we've experienced it. We must remember that if there is a shared burden on the part of those who want a better future, it is the burden that we all have to imagine our world, to think about what it should and can be. So when people ask me why the political right is so good at messaging, I remind them that it isn't so much that they're good at messaging, but that their message is rooted in familiar iconography. It is nostalgia writ large.

We are trying to bring about something altogether new, an idea that we must collectively buy into to make it a reality. And unfortunately, it is easy for ideas to get muddied in translation. Think of single-payer health care—we have never seen it in this country, so when we're asked to buy into this new system, it requires a lot of imagination. It requires us to envision an entire system and structure that has never existed here. So it is no wonder why, for some, conjuring up images of a concrete past during which they benefited handsomely would be attractive. On the left, we have a tendency to veer into squabbles over the image of the future we are fighting for, even when we are essentially fighting for the same thing. And that's because shared imaginations are difficult to manage.

In order to imagine, especially in the midst of trauma, our work is to name the constraints up front and then ignore them. This will be a challenge because they are often so potent, so present. But we can name and expose our limitations, and then work around them. Imagination is often thought of as a soft, feel-good aspect of the work of justice, but without it, we will never win.

WHEN THOSE OF US who have come from marginalized communities and/or are engaged in the work of social justice are paving a way forward, we need to figure out how to resolve the internal tensions that will necessarily arise in order to do our best work. Thus we need a compass. Since the protests began in Ferguson, I have thought about the role of the church in the work of social justice and how belief factors into our collective work. In many ways, the civil rights movement was born out of institutions—largely churches and schools. But when we took to the streets in St. Louis, it was the result of an organic infrastructure and not the work of organizations or institutions. Even so, there were local pastors—Traci Blackmon, Renita Lamkin, Tommie Pierson Jr., and Starsky Wilson, to name a few—who were pivotal, as they both protested and assisted protesters in organizing. One day, when Brittany, Netta, and I were traveling, we even called Pastor Blackmon so that she could pray over us on the phone as we were heading into a challenging situation in another city.

I will never forget when Pastor Renita stood between protesters and police on a night that was particularly tense—we thought the police had killed a young man and were hiding their actions as they blocked us from entering the church parking lot—and as she stood between the two camps, she prayed out loud in a firm and warm tone. I'll never forget the chills I got as we all watched her pray. The police immediately eased up, as did the protesters. It immediately changed the tone of the tension. And Pastor Pierson and Pastor Wilson repeatedly opened up their churches to create space for a range of events, meetings, actions, and to host visitors who were coming to assist the protesters.

The access to resources, the stability of the infrastructure, and the deep sense of moral courage were factors that made the church an important part of the protest landscape in the end, even though they were not the central part of the protest ecosystem.

Even if people were not regular churchgoers or especially religious otherwise, the church still held an important role in the way they thought about the black community. For this reason, it was disappointing when churches turned us away or called the police on us or were simply absent during the unrest. And for some, challenging these churches was off limits. It reminded me that the black church, in many ways, is about more than faith per se; it is also a model of black power. Thus, to challenge the churches was to challenge long-standing pillars of black power. But to us, the presence of power also means the presence of responsibility.

I THINK I GAINED an understanding of God and faith during the movement. On the first night that I drove to Ferguson, I got tired. I was in a small town in Iowa and I knew that I needed to stop for a nap, even if a short one. If I kept on driving, I was certain that I was going to run off the road. So I tried to find a landmark where I could sleep in my car for an hour or so. I found a church. I got some clothes out of the trunk, reclined the chair, and used the clothes as a pillow. I didn't know it then, but the church would continue to serve as an anchor in the most challenging times during the protests. On the first night of the curfew, I got separated from all of my friends, my phones died, and I ended up on Chambers Street, out of which there was no outlet—all the connected streets were dead ends. And while I was walking, trying to find someone who could help, a man waved to me. I couldn't make him out right away, but he was a pastor, and the building behind him was a church. I went inside and joined others, who, like me, had become stranded and needed a place of refuge for the night.

By and by, I began to believe that I was doing the work that I was meant to do, and that as long as I stayed true to my convictions, I would be okay. It was an understanding of God that helped me to think more about accountability. I had heard people mostly use accountability as a weapon to challenge people who did not adhere to their ideas or actions, or who made decisions contrary to the loudest voices. But it was in understanding faith better that I came to understand accountability as the quality of one's adherence to one's own values, beliefs, and commitments.

I often think of God in the context of activism as reminding us of our moral courage—of being a compass as we navigate key moral issues, those of good and evil and those of justice. Moral courage is the courage summoned because you are firmly rooted in the righteousness of the task at hand. And I think that faith is often an easier facilitator of moral courage than is its absence. But in this moment, the call for moral courage is received differently, as the movement has not been rooted in a belief in God. And thus religious belief has not been the anchor it once was. And I have been thinking about what it means to win in the absence of a belief in God. When I read Dr. Martin Luther King Jr.'s words, "winning" is so closely tied to an ultimate "win" that is salvific. And I think that there is something particularly powerful about anchoring an idea of victory to a world that has not existed before. It keeps the focus on the possible, on the things that we know to be true but are yet unseen, like freedom.

In a complicated world, we know that the institution of the church isn't the only moral compass, but that ideas of good and evil come from many places—Storm taught me that before I ever understood any teachings from church. It will continue to be important that we validate the many ways that people come to navigate this world with regard to morality, especially when the church hasn't been an open or safe space to so many for so long. I found faith in the streets and in seeing a set of churches live their commitment to justice.

I learned more about God and faith in the protests. But Storm raised me.

SEVEN

Taking the Truth Everywhere

*Working the cracks within the system,
however, requires learning to speak multiple
languages of power convincingly.*

—PATRICIA HILL COLLINS

The West Wing is small, smaller than it appears in shows like *House of Cards* or *Scandal*. The ceilings are low, the hallways are narrow, and the lone bathroom stall off the main corridor is a reminder that the layout is from another era—that it is truly an old American building. I was reminded that some of our traditions are old America as well. We are a nation of theoretical equals, but President Obama's chair was the largest in the Roosevelt Room and it was in the middle of the table, as is perhaps expected for the leader of the free world. It was cold outside, as this meeting was on February 18, 2016. But it was warm in the West Wing.

I received an emailed invitation to join a group of activists to meet with President Obama in late January 2016 in the first intergenerational meeting of civil rights leaders ever hosted by a president. There was a mandatory call with a White

House staffer in advance of the meeting. I took the call from home and shared the line with an activist from Chicago and another young leader from the NAACP. The facilitator explained that we would meet with senior White House staff and then with President Obama; we would give introductory statements, then proceed to ask him questions, which we were requested but not required to provide in advance of the meeting.

I was ready to meet the president. His administration had, after all, been slow to pressure police departments to change their practices by withholding their funding from the Department of Justice; and they had been slower than we expected to condemn police violence and validate our cause. I knew that no meeting would bring back any of the people whose deaths had brought us to the streets. But it could help prevent future trauma.

Our future will be the result of choices we are now making, and thus it is incumbent on us to engage with the political process. Of course, politicians are rarely the saviors we want them to be. And this is often less of an indictment of them and more of a reminder that they are still human, working within structures we've created—both of which are flawed and imperfect. Though flawed and imperfect, they can move us tangibly closer to freedom—*or* move us further away. And while politicians come and go, the citizenry remains. Our greatest responsibility in all of politics, then, is active citizenship: protesting, voting, running for office, working to address issues in one's local community, and so forth.

I am constantly reminding myself that the goal of protest is *progress*, not simply more protest. Protest, though not the solution, is a precursor to the solution. It creates space that would otherwise not exist, and forces conversations and topics that have been long ignored into the public sphere. It illuminates what our country would rather forget. Protest remains necessary in a country with such ingrained systemic inequity and in which the traditional mechanisms of power have not often benefited marginalized communities without direct pressure. In agreeing to meet with President Obama, we recognized that our commitment to this work begins with protest, but that it does not end there.

I committed to what would be the first of several meetings with President Obama and his team to tell the truth and to listen. I was hopeful that he would hear us out, and when he spoke I was reminded that his power, while both structural and systemic, was also a power of narrative-shaping and storytelling.

He gave us all a chance to speak before offering reflections on the things that he'd heard. He explained that he would move forward with nominating the next member of the Supreme Court; that the administration was working, with others, to address the mens rea issue in the context of current sentencing reform legislation; and that while there was significant work yet to be done, much work had been done already, and we were in a better position than we had been in before. This was a consistent refrain of his in those final days of his administration—that despite the distance ahead, we'd covered much ground already. It was a long meeting, having run over its allotted time; when it did, he noted that he would only have time to engage the younger civil rights leaders, and we continued our conversation.

When we met with him again four months later, the tone and tenor of these issues had grown even more severe. I had been arrested in Baton Rouge shortly before I met with Obama for the second time, in what would be the longest non–national security meeting he participated in while in office. There were no reporters in the room during either of our meetings; no cameras or tweets were allowed. This was an opportunity for genuine conversations about reform—not a press conference or a photo opportunity. Nevertheless, there were calls from within the protest community and from without accusing us of political grandstanding and labeling the activists in attendance as sellouts. I did not agree with the Obama administration on every issue. I still cringe when I think of him using the term "thugs" to describe protesters in Baltimore—and I told him as much. But if we only meet with people with whom we totally agree, then progress will never happen. And if the goal is real, lasting change, then we will have to take the fight everywhere—and that included the Obama White House.

I have heard people decry "reform" as a weakening of the

spirit of protest. But this is simply false. Reform is an acknowledgment that we can change things today that will improve people's lives in both the short and long terms. Ensuring that those who are incarcerated can call their families at as little cost as possible is good for people *today*. Creating access to books for families in schools that have historically struggled to teach literacy is good for families *today*. Developing a strategy to ensure that black families have access to more information about financial literacy is good for families *today*. These are not wholesale systemic changes, but they move us in the right direction.

Reform is not a concession or an unwillingness to plan toward larger political goals—such as fundamentally altering our conception of democracy or of the two-party political system. Reform is not a reshuffling of the status quo or political musical chairs that serves as a performance of substance with no impact. But we must work to change the conditions of our lived reality *today*, while maintaining a commitment to changing the core power structures that led to the conditions that caused us to fight in the first place. It concerns me that those who decry reform would sacrifice people's immediate well-being while holding out for an "ideal" plan that wouldn't begin to see returns for half a century—when the communities that need it most today are already dead.

In meeting with elected officials, whether it was the president, a mayor, or a state senator, we kept to a set of core commitments: first, a seat at the table requires that you bring the truth with you while recognizing that, second, you are not the only person who can bring the truth, and, last, that you work to keep the door open for others. We met with President Obama in an attempt to influence an agenda at the national level that could potentially help create a model for states and cities to follow in leveraging the power of the federal government to hold police departments accountable.

THE TENSION between purity and participation is real. I felt it when I ran for office, when—despite growing up in the city, working as a youth organizer as a teenager in the city, launching an after-school center for middle-grades—I was branded an outsider by detractors who felt that I sought office without gaining their permission first. And the facts didn't matter because the activist community was as fervent as the political establishment about maintaining its gatekeeper role. Moreover, before the election of Donald Trump, there was a widespread belief that all activism happens outside of systems and structures. So the mere notion of me seeking office upset many people. I was unprepared for leftist publications to deride my decision to run for office by claiming that it wasn't my decision at all, and that I must have been a pawn or tool of the white elite. But I got a keen sense of the way that supposed ideological purity can change the political landscape with mixed effects, especially inside the activist community.

Running for office is like basic organizing—there is no

substitute for connecting with people, and relationships, especially one-on-one, matter. We raised three hundred thousand dollars in about sixty days, knocked on thirty thousand doors in that same time frame, had donors from every state and the third highest number of donors from Baltimore City, and pushed each of the candidates to release more detailed platforms than had existed before. One of the reasons I ran in the first place is that I realized that, with roughly eighty days until the primary election, almost no one then running had a robust platform. It was as if they had simply taken for granted that they might prevail on account of their name alone. I knew that our city deserved more, that we deserved leadership with a vision and a plan, and I knew that I could offer one.

Ideological purity is not a political goal. Nevertheless, the desire for it is strong, especially among those who know that it is an implausible reality. Politics, the decision-making process that helps to shape the way we interact with our communities and vice versa, is necessarily one of compromise, as ideas, experiences, and plans regularly come into conflict with one another. To assert that politics is compromise is not to suggest that we should ever compromise our core values. It is to suggest, however, that the process requires that we understand that the people with whom we engage have different experiences and ideas that will influence how they make decisions.

There are some who believe that we should never engage those in seats of power, but this is an ideological stance and not a political stance. Our daily lives are shaped by large systems and structures—from trash collections to stoplights to parking tickets to schools to prisons. Not to engage the people whose decisions and choices shape our lives is to misunderstand our own agency and potential for impact. If engaging people in seats of power has the potential to positively impact the lives of the people we claim to serve, then engagement as a political choice is important. During the 2016 presidential election, some people refused to vote because they felt their vote didn't matter, or they didn't like the candidates, or they felt that the president didn't influence their daily lives. And there were others, mostly elites, who told people that they shouldn't vote because the candidates were different sides of the same coin, as if there weren't marked differences between the candidates. I publicly supported Hillary Clinton in an op-ed in the *Washington Post* and received an intense backlash. But I believed Donald Trump; I took him at his word. I felt like the choice was real and clear, and I had to use my platform to try to influence as many people as possible. Unfortunately, it seems again that in this tension between ideology and outcomes, a fealty to ideology won out to devastating effect. Others would say things like "we can afford to lose an election," positing options that exist only in a theoretical world.

To be sure, there is a tension associated with engaging a power structure that we are simultaneously working to change. Why engage something that you are trying to dismantle, or something that you are trying to change so fundamentally that it will not be the same afterward? We engage the system for three reasons: first, where it's possible to organize citizens to use collective action and power to make the choices in lieu of those in traditional power, we must do so; second, people inside of systems often need external pressure in order to push an agenda aligned with our values; and finally, we use every tool at our disposal to influence change, noting that there are often unlikely pockets of support that would not exist if we did not have a broad engagement strategy.

Those who are unwilling to embrace this tension, who see themselves as taking a "radical" stance, do so at the expense of having a politics that challenges the status quo. A radicalism that at its heart is about dismantling the status quo in favor of an unimagined "better future" is not in fact radicalism, but actually a cold detachment from reality itself. To be radical implies having an idea in juxtaposition to the dominant one. The absence of an idea is not radicalism.

We can acknowledge the imperfections of the choices that are sometimes in front of us while maintaining a focus on the consequences of action (or inaction). Our focus, indeed our North Star, is always a concern for improving lives, not for how we will maintain our reputation as radicals or revolutionaries—as if that reputation alone will prevent deportations, end police violence, or promote economic equity.

This too is the tension between popular uses of reform and revolution. Reform is the realm of immediate change—we put something into action today and see the results tomorrow.

Revolution is the idea that there are deep, structural, and systemic choices to be made that will lead to larger-scale changes. So ensuring that people who are incarcerated have adequate meals is reform to some, as it will mean working within a system to press for change that at the end of the day will negligibly impact the fight for the end of mass incarceration. But people who are incarcerated should have healthy meals, right? Yes, of course they should. This is an example of the tension that exists when theory meets practice. The role of the protester need not be akin to that of the general: leading a complicated strategy that knowingly, if remorsefully, sacrifices people in pursuit of the win. When we see that lives can be improved through actions we feasibly take, we must take them.

Rightly applied, reform includes effective policies for improvement; wrongly applied, it simply makes cosmetic changes that work to uphold the status quo. After the death of Alton Sterling, the Baton Rouge police chief asked for higher salaries for officers in an apparent effort to improve the quality of the workforce through higher compensation, as if that would lead to lower rates of police violence by his officers. That is an example of bad "reform."

WE KNEW THAT it would be important to work to influence the platforms of some of the nominees during the 2016 presidential election, too. I tweeted to both Bernie Sanders and Hillary Clinton requesting meetings; both replied that they would meet with us and they did. In setting up the meetings, we aimed to invite activists from across the country so that a range of perspectives were represented. We knew that the meeting needed to include more than just Brittany, Sam, Netta, and me. After both of our initial meetings, I wrote a post summarizing the main policy points that arose.

We met with Bernie Sanders first, on September 16, 2015. In this meeting, we reviewed his expansive platform that addressed criminal justice and other issues of racial justice. Though his platform was impressive in its range, we had questions about its depth. In preparation for the meeting, we had a conference call to ensure that every participant had a working understanding of the ideas that he had proposed thus far. One of the things that caught us by surprise during the conversation with Bernie was when we began to talk about mass incarceration. He suggested that the police were policing black communities disproportionately because the majority of drug users were African American. The line went silent as we all tried to digest what we'd just heard, certain that he had more to say on the matter, but he didn't. We addressed his comment in our response; we explained that his statement was totally untrue and that such thinking has consequences for the way policy is set. When his statement became public, Bernie's team released a response: "While I clearly misspoke and had more to learn with regard to the causes of this problem, we all came to the meeting understanding what is absolutely true: the criminal justice system is broken and disproportionately arrests and jails African Americans." We continued to connect with his policy team to influence his campaign's platform, and it eventually gained more depth from all of the pushes within the social justice community—depth that matched its broad scope. This meeting was a reminder that even the most well-intentioned political leaders need to be challenged on core issues and that it is critical that we understand the ideas and beliefs that form the basis for the legislation they propose or support.

We met with Hillary Clinton on two occasions: once before she became the nominee, on October 9, 2015, and again after. In the first meeting, she had not yet released her platform, so we took all of her public statements and essentially made a platform out of it so that everyone in the meeting would be prepared to ask questions that were informed by her previous public statements and stances. That meeting was unremarkable; she was noncommittal about most issues, noting that they would be addressed in her platform upon its eventual release. We'd spoken with her policy team prior to both meetings in order to influence the platform, too. But when we met with her in Cleveland after she'd become the nominee, she was the most candid I'd ever experienced her. It was just Brittany Packnett and me in this meeting; we'd asked Hillary's team to record it so that we could broadcast it later and they'd agreed. One of the things we asked her about was the part of her platform that supported an increase in police training, and we said that while that is generally a good thing, the police do not need any more money. And she fully agreed. She then paused and explained that she knew that while the police needed more training, that the money could be diverted to community groups and other practitioners and that the police were already well-funded. She noted, and we agreed, that this might actually have an impact. I was surprised to hear her rationale and her candor. Despite assurances, her team did not release the video of the meeting. If they had allowed its release, I think people would have seen her in a completely different light. The entire conversation was illuminative in a way that I frankly didn't expect. Hillary's platform was tight and focused on large-scale solutions, and we kept pushing her to increase its range.

That I fell short in running for office, or a president I admired fell short of the actions I sought, or even that the candidate I supported lost, does not dissuade me from the notion that engagement matters. We must not only tell the truth everywhere—in the ballot box, in city hall and in the White House, on social media, in the streets and in classrooms, and at the dinner table—we must also fight for that truth to be heard and acted upon.

I Can Remember.

EIGHT

I Can Remember Her Now Without Sadness

And now, each night I count the stars,
And each night I get the same number.
And when they will not come to be counted,
I count the holes they leave.

—AMIRI BARAKA

She left when I was three. And every time I see her now, I want to ask her why she left. I want to ask her if she thought about me as much as I felt her absence. I want to ask her if she loved us, because I've never thought about love as leaving, not this type of love. I want to tell her that a part of me began to prepare for people to choose to leave me one day, like she did. And that I stopped believing in unconditional love when she left. I want to tell her about how hard it was to hear people talk about their mothers, and to sit silently and not let the pain show on my face.

But I've never asked her why she left. And I've never told her the things on my mind. Because I could always see the pain in her eyes. And I wouldn't be another thing in this world that broke her, even if I was broken by her.

It took me a while to learn not to respond to pain with pain. I think I'm still learning.

I used to call her Mommy Joan when I was younger. I don't remember exactly when I dropped the "Mommy" part and began to call her Joan, but I think it was when I was eight or so. It just didn't feel honest any other way. And we never saw her anyway, so it wasn't like I was going to get in trouble.

It wasn't until I was an adult that my father explained that her parents used to put her to sleep with alcohol. In some ways, addiction was chosen for her before she made any choices of her own. She'd been battling it her entire life and was in recovery when my older sister, TeRay, and I were born. Both of our parents were.

But one night, one of my mother's friends invited her to a party; she used, and never looked back. There was no custody battle; she left willingly. She told my father that we'd have a better life with him. And the rest, I guess, is history.

She reentered my life when I was thirty. I had only seen her a few times around the holidays before then. I always remembered her as a slim woman, and over the years the drugs had taken her from slim to slight and sharp around the edges. But something was markedly different this time. She'd gained just the smallest amount of weight, negligible really, but what she lacked in pounds she seemed to have in pride as she told me, "I'm gaining weight." Despite the many years that had passed between her moments of sobriety when I was a child, I could remember enough of what she was truly like to know that the person in front of me was done using. What I couldn't decide was what her sobriety now meant to me. How do you make up for so much lost time? So many lost memories?

I had many mothers in my life, but Joan was not one of them. Nanny, my great-grandmother, filled the biggest void, helping to raise me and TeRay from our earliest years until the beginning of middle school. I talked about Nanny with one of my friends recently, and I realized that I don't talk about her much anymore. It's not because she didn't play an incredibly important role in my life, but precisely because she played such an important role in my life.

When I was younger, I used to randomly wake up in tears, because I thought that Nanny was going to die. I have no clue where the idea came from, but I remember those nights waking up crying. And she would assure me that she'd be here tomorrow. Even as a kid I realized that she was much older than my father. And I think it was a combination of her frequent doctor visits and self-administered daily insulin shots that made me think she would die.

When she died during my senior year in college, it felt like she took all the music in the world with her. She was one of the first people who I knew loved me. It was sometimes a tough love, a love rooted in rules and structure. But it was a love that I understood and that I knew was there to protect me. In the years since her death, I've realized that I don't actively remember her as much as I once did. And the reason is partly that it's a bit too painful sometimes to think about her absence, especially as so much in my world continues to change. I would've loved to call her about the protests and hear her tell me where she was during all of the events of the civil rights movement. I would've wanted her around to guide me through the relationships I've had or the plans that I've made, acting as a sounding board as I became more civically engaged. In her absence, I've chosen to simply focus on other things, to remember other things.

My grandmother is another mother. She's always called me D-R to distinguish my name from my sister's. I can still hear her yelling "D-R!" from across that big house, asking me to get more ice for her water, to change the channel on the TV, or to go get the phone in the other room.

And Robin became the mother I didn't know I needed until she entered my life, being like a friend, mentor, and parent all in one. We met when I was a youth organizer with Baltimore's Safe and Sound Campaign, as a teenager, and she took me under her wing and both believed in me and challenged me in ways that few adults had done up to that point in my life. She always loved me like a hug—a little bit of love and a little bit of pressure.

Even though I had other mothers, I had to learn not to be bitter on Mother's Day, to still be joyful on a day when I couldn't celebrate like everyone else. And over time the joy wasn't necessarily feigned anymore. I was happy for the other kids and the other adults. I had come to peace with the what and how of our family. But now she's back.

When Joan returned, I wanted to just pick up from where we left off, build a new relationship and just move forward. I'm able to tell myself that there were other people who filled those voids, who were there for the birthdays and celebrations, who gave me encouragement when times were hard, who taught me the shapes and sizes of love. I'm still grappling with the tension between Joan's absence and the suddenness of her presence, and what my responsibility is, if any, as a son right now. Because I've always been her son, even if I felt like I didn't actually have a mother. I think so, anyway.

THE PAST IS what we call the actions and events that have already happened. Memory, however, is a choice. History is our *re*-membering, our literal rejoining of our memories, influenced by our biases, desires, and goals. It is our interpretation of everything that has taken place before the present, and the effects of those actions and events. Our interpretation and understanding of the past shape our choices in the present. Memory, and therefore history, is always an exercise in power and choice.

To re-member is also a political act, a process that is informed by our own proximity to and away from power, and that shapes our proximity to and away from power. We often think of politics as a grand enterprise, rooted in elections and laws, but it often shows up in our homes, our communities, and our relationships in more mundane disguises.

Politics is fundamentally about power, and it is always

relational—that is, it can only be understood as something between people, systems, and interests. But politics is not simply about power in a traditional sense. Politics is about power through process: band together to elect a party to majority; elect an official to put forward a bill. Power is the ability to influence the decision-making process. But the relationship of politics to power is rooted in the more fundamental idea that individuals have their own innate power and that politics is really the exercise of many individuals' collective power or an individual's attempt to change the collective. Politics as we understand it now is just the most visible indication that people are participating in the community. Many people think they've never been involved in "politics" because they've been conditioned to think of the political process as beyond their abilities.

So when we talk about "building power" it is shorthand for two things: first, helping people recognize that they can influence a given decision-making process to achieve a defined goal; and second, assembling a critical mass of people who are equipped to act in concert with each other. But the way that people think about their own power, about the power of their community, about the possibility of change, is influenced by how we remember the past.

We tend to gravitate toward an understanding of the past divorced from the idea that individuals, or groups of individuals, at each critical moment made a series of decisions that shapes our present. It's in this way that memory can be a tool for *X* or a weapon for *Y*, depending on how it is wielded and to what end.

We make different decisions about what we remember, about how we tell the stories of the past and their impact, depending on whether the event is one of trauma or triumph, one of victory or defeat, one of joy or pain. We make different decisions, too, based on where we stood then—whether we had power or were fighting for power; whether we were thriving or surviving; fighting, fleeing, or standing our ground.

The claim to an objective, comprehensive recollection of events is a ruse put forth by those who would have their version of events seen as the sole interpretation. But to pretend that there is only one interpretation of the past is to participate in fiction.

We can remember the civil rights movement by focusing on prominent straight men, as has been done for decades. But we know that a more complete way to re-member it is to discuss the vital contributions of women and members of the LGBTQ community. And we can choose to do this. The same is true for other events in history. Take the Civil War, for example. When the school boards in Texas mandate that the Civil War be described as the "War Between the States," and that textbooks should explicitly describe the motivation for the war as "protecting states' rights," that is a choice. They have chosen to remember the past in a way that ignores the impact and persistence of white supremacy as an organizing principle in the Confederacy and as a pretext for war.

Memory serves as its own form of resistance, its own challenge to the forces that seduce us into romanticizing the past or overcelebrating progress and believing that it has unlocked the more just future.

Each generation reckons with the past and the ways in which events from an earlier time inform their present. The poll tax likely felt progressive when compared to slavery. I remember seeing the images of water hoses aimed at children during the civil rights movement when I was in school. I remember seeing Rodney King being beaten on TV. I remember hearing my great-grandmother and grandparents talk about the unrest following Martin Luther King Jr.'s murder. I remember learning about Stonewall.

We have been told that *that* America was in the past, that we had gotten beyond that America. I was told that the overt attitudes of white supremacy and racism were relics of another time. And when there wasn't a mechanism to share information quickly that wasn't filtered by a mainstream media source, it sometimes felt like the worst of days was in the past too.

History is a potent tool and can be used to aid in the work of either domination or liberation, as it is both the proxy by which we gauge progress and the point of departure for learning and imagination. Those who use history as a tool for domination require ample distance between the past and the present in order to demonstrate progress; they will even artificially create this distance when necessary. Domination also remembers the past either as acts of innocence or necessity on behalf of those benefiting from domination, and as acts of defiance, inferiority, or pathology on behalf of the oppressed.

Domination requires willful forgetting or deliberate misremembering, notably of the enduring nature of itself, and it exploits our collective desire for progress. It plays on our desire to make wins seem larger, more significant or permanent than they truly were, or to conflate sacrifice and effort with fundamental change.

History is meant to guide, not prescribe. It is important that we not play into the I-know-history-therefore-I-know-the-future trope that I have encountered among people who professionally teach and study history or politics. I understand the sentiment: there are times when we quite rightly invoke history to challenge behavior that we suspect will be damaging, because, as the saying goes, we have been there before.

The further we seem to move from a given event or way of life, the easier it is for us to believe that the distance from historically damaging events is itself progress. This, what I call the false distance of history, is the incremental progress spread out over decades that undercuts our efforts at radical progress measured out over years. The false distance of history aims to deceive us into believing that the trauma of racism and injustice is in our past. It plays on our desire for a memory of the past that makes sense and feels good. The false distance of history provides the vehicle for monuments celebrating traitors who rebelled in order to preserve the institution of slavery to be left standing.

But those of us who live *in* this trauma know the difference between progress and distance. We know that no matter how much we want to satisfy our desire for progress, we must do the work of countering false claims of advancement that complicate our understanding of what true gains actually look like, and of highlighting the consistency between the past and present.

The actions that have historically been markers of racism have changed. But the ideas that have allowed racism to flourish in whatever nuanced form it takes have remained. And the way we measure progress, namely by our proximity to or away from enslavement and lynching, allows racism to flourish further still. The absence of enslavement and lynching does not signal the presence of equality and justice.

I, like many others, should not know the difference between pepper spray and pepper balls, the sting of Mace, the sharpness of tear gas, the pitch of sound cannons, or the impact of smoke bombs—but I do. I remember these not to glorify trauma, but simply because they happened. And I remember because forgetting may seduce me into believing in a progress that has not yet arrived.

Those initial days of the movement, and of protest, still show up in my dreams, still inform the ways in which I think about coalition building, about organizing, and about systemic change. I think they will always be with me. For a time they haunted me, but not anymore.

We have a responsibility to remember—a responsibility to

those who fought before us and a responsibility to understand progress as authentic growth.

I think about Joan every day—not necessarily because I am thinking about her presence or absence, but because I am thinking about my worthiness and my ability to be loved. The choices she made have impacted the way I think about my own future and my own possibilities, my own worth and my own value. It took me a while to re-member her in a way that was not solely rooted in loss and lack, in a way that was not about absence but about the difficulty of making a decision that would forever impact the lives of two young children and her husband.

I can now remember Joan without sadness. But that was a choice and it was a process to get here. I'll have to ask her one day why she left. I need to build the courage to have the tough conversation about the past so that I can better understand how we can build a future together, if we are ever to have one. I think she wants to have a relationship now and I'm trying to make sense of that, to see how to make that happen in a way that doesn't set me up to be hurt again.

I am mindful that we re-member pain and trauma differently than we remember joy and triumph. When we remember pain, we are trying to protect ourselves and cope. We are trying to order the memories in ways that will allow us to make it to tomorrow and to the day after tomorrow. In trauma, we often traffic in denial—not in an attempt to be subversive, but because it is a way to ease the pain, to simply act as if something didn't happen. There were times when I'd convinced myself that Joan hadn't left, that something else happened. And when that didn't keep, I convinced myself that I had other "mothers." But I can't run from the fact that the woman who gave birth to me chose to leave. This is simply a fact.

I wonder sometimes if in the way I can remember Joan without sadness there will come a day that I can look back on this America without the pain and trauma we've endured being so present. I too am often seduced by the false distance of history. I want to believe in a progress so sweeping that I can ignore how present the trauma still is. And sometimes the false distance keeps me sane. In the way that I had to *re*-remember Joan, I have had to *re*-remember my relationship with America. I'd like to think that I created a space for Joan and me to reconnect, and that we did reconnect was because she was making a space for me too in whatever way made the most sense to her, and that our spaces finally overlapped.

What we remember and how we re-member it shapes our future, shapes the way we move in the world. And memory is always a choice.

I have agency in how I remember Joan as time goes by and how I tell that story, to the world and to myself. We have agency about how we remember our collective past and how we allow those stories to be told. I hope that the truth, in all its thorniness, is what we remember.

NINE

The Friend That's Always Awake

But surely to tell these tall tales and others
like them would be to speed the myth,
the wicked lie, that the past is always
tense and the future, perfect.

—ZADIE SMITH

On a hot spring day in 1955 in Montgomery, Alabama, fifteen-year-old Claudette Colvin did not know that she was making history. The people making history rarely do. But she knew that up until then, she had been presented with a false choice: either she could remain silent in the face of oppression, or she could challenge the status quo and become a martyr in her turn. But she knew that there was a third option, as there often is—there was a way to engage in resistance that could lead to a more lasting fundamental change. She was on a bus on her way home from school when it became crowded to the point that all the seats designated for white people were full. Inevitably, she was asked to vacate her seat for a white person who wanted it, and she refused. Her words describing the day she refused to stand still echo:

One of them said to the driver in a very angry tone, "Who is it?" The motorman pointed at me. I heard him say, "That's nothing new . . . I've had trouble with that 'thing' before." He called me a "thing." They came to me and stood over me and one said, "Aren't you going to get up?" I said, "No, sir." He shouted "Get up" again. I started crying, but I felt even more defiant. I kept saying over and over, in my high-pitched voice, "It's my constitutional right to sit here as much as that lady. I paid my fare, it's my constitutional right!" I knew I was talking back to a white policeman, but I had had enough.*

Colvin, along with Aurelia Browder, Mary Louise Smith, and Susie McDonald were the plaintiffs in *Browder v. Gayle*, the Supreme Court case that led to the desegregation of public transportation. Colvin's story is too often a missing story, the story of a fifteen-year-old soon-to-be-unwed mother swapped for that of Rosa Parks, who, with seemingly less baggage, was a better fit to be the face of a movement. It took a Supreme Court case for her experience to be documented, for an author writing years later to tell her story. I think of her often when I think about the promise of the social media tools we have

---

* Philip Hoose, *Claudette Colvin: Twice Toward Justice*. New York: Farrar, Straus and Giroux, 2009.

at our disposal. What about her story would have been told differently had it been shown live, or documented via text in real time? What of her fullness as a person, coupled with the bravery of her confrontation and its implications, would we have been forced to engage?

PROFESSOR JO ANN ROBINSON knew that the conditions in Montgomery had reached a tipping point. In the middle of the night, she made a stencil and pressed over thirty-five thousand flyers that she, along with two of her students, distributed to high school students in Montgomery, Alabama, thus sparking the Montgomery bus boycott. In describing the feeling of victory when the bus boycott was successful, she noted:

> We felt that we were somebody, that somebody had
> to listen to us, that we had forced the white man to
> give what we knew was a part of our own citizen-
> ship . . . and so we had won that. And if you have
> never had the feeling to feel that this is not the other
> man's country and you are an alien in it, but that this
> is your country, too, then you don't know what I'm
> talking about.*

* Jo Ann Robinson, interview by Llew Smith and Judy Richardson, *Eyes on the Prize*, August 27, 1979.

Hers is another missing story. And while we can imagine the ability of social media to tell the story, one can only imagine what someone like Professor Robinson would have done with a series of tools that could instantly engage audiences far and wide, audiences not tethered to sheets of paper.

HISTORY IS THE ACCUMULATION of our stories. Stories help us make sense of the choices we've made, of the choices we're afraid to make, and of those choices made for us that define our lives. There is a reason we tell stories. The world we live in doesn't always make sense. Or it is so unpredictable that we need tools, devices, and images to help us process its pace and flow. We tell stories to remember, to pass on what we've learned, to nurture the thread of progress. Our stories give meaning to moments and birth new ones. They organize what is exceptional in ways that are understandable.

As our stories were once passed on generation to generation via word of mouth, then written and read, then seen on screen, the internet has now changed our proximity to each other's thoughts, putting us in unprecedented closeness with one another minute to minute. We now digitally chronicle the mundane and paramount aspects of our lives in ways that few predicted, and we are still coming to understand the consequences.

Perhaps because of this, the world feels as if it has moved quicker in the past decade than in all the years preceding it. The stakes feel as high as any I've ever lived through. In a political and social climate in which the fabric of our democracy has been laid bare, in all of its fragility, and the scaling back of hard-fought wins seems imminent, there's a palpable urgency in the information swirling about us.

Sometimes the speed with which all of this information moves is our friend. It allows us to organize, to respond, to anticipate, and to plan better than we could have in its absence. It lets us discover and share new voices, perspectives, ideas. Other times, speed is our foe. Like a game of telephone, information can move so quickly that we gain a good story—at times the story we want to believe—at the expense of the truth. We're in a time when fact and fiction, truth and lies, move with equal speed. And narratives can travel so far from the truth so quickly that we can become stuck between remembering and correcting. And too often lies outlive the truth.

The narrative gatekeepers have fallen. Tweets can lead to revolution. Instagram videos can give rise to careers. Facebook posts can register more voters than any party. And people can access and reinforce the stories they want to believe, and find a community of willing believers, in ways that are unparalleled in our history. The digital landscape has enhanced both our ability to tell stories and our responsibility to tell the truth.

In no uncertain terms, Twitter saved our lives. If it were not for Twitter, the elected leaders in Ferguson and in Missouri would have tried to convince you that we did not exist, that there were not thousands of us in the street night after night, refusing to be silent. We never had to wait for the newspaper or the nightly news to capture the events of the night; we could capture them ourselves. Critics of the movement have accused us of "chasing cameras" during the protests. I have to remind them that *we were the cameras!* For those of us who were there, we saw the power of social media platforms to allow us to do things that were unimaginable before, like moving crowds of five thousand people or mapping out actions across an entire city. The largest and most coordinated of all of our actions during the protests was Occupy SLU (St. Louis University), which was the brainchild of Dhoruba Shakur and Tribe X and executed by Kayla Reed, Leon Kemp, and a few others. On that night, we moved two crowds of approximately three thousand people to break a police barricade and to occupy a university all via Twitter and Vine.

It's common to hear talk of social media as a random by-product of "real" organizing that can only happen offline. It's a sentiment most commonly expressed by people who simply weren't there or never experienced the transformative impact that these tools had on our lives—some of whom purport to speak for a new type of organizing today. We used these tools to enhance our organizing and activism, not as substitutes for either.

We often think of storytelling in the oral tradition or in the written tradition, in books and articles. We think of the author telling us their account and then responses to that account. But the protests in Ferguson were the proof point that collective storytelling is possible, that many people all talking about the same event in real time is another way, a powerful way, to tell a story. It was no longer a matter of whether you trusted one person's account or the news platform, but whether you were tuned in while thousands of people explained the world they were experiencing. Collective storytelling, though, is fraught with the same perils as every other mode of storytelling—sometimes the collective can fix itself to a narrative rooted more in imagination than fact. Russia's ability to generate false stories that were seen by millions of individuals during the 2016 presidential election is a testament to this fact.

When falsehoods become accepted thought, there are real consequences for how we understand the world. We have a responsibility, and daily make a choice, to unpack and challenge the ideas that are carried in stories, to refine and inspect our language, and to correct false narratives despite the cost or discomfort. The things we upvote and the things we downvote, what we choose to click on (and not), and, most important, what we choose to share, now determine "truth."

We have not always had a shared experience to highlight the danger of the false narrative. We do now. "Post-truth," the Oxford Dictionaries 2016 Word of the Year, is defined as "relating to or denoting circumstances in which objective facts are less influential in shaping public opinion than appeals to emotion and personal belief." In the past year, we have seen the impact that a post-truth culture can have on both the lived reality and the psyche of communities. It's tempting to think we have also seen segments of America *choose* between a good story and the truth, with the good story often being one that appeals to emotion and personal belief despite the facts. But in truth we are all guilty of this to a certain extent. Those less educated among us may be more susceptible to it, but the desire to believe the story that aligns with what we already feel to be true is natural. Sometimes it is real work to get to the truth.

Trump is an excellent, insidious storyteller who thrives in the false narrative. Of course, he is not the first or only politician to take advantage of the ignorance of the American body politic, or to play on stereotypes or long-standing divisions. He is, however, the first president who has truly plied this trade using the tools of social media. His delivery of intentional disinformation* preys on his opponents' steadfast commitment to the moral high ground even if it leads to their destruction; the public's belief in a basic level of integrity; the collective lack of knowledge about governmental minutiae; and the latent racism that still undergirds so much of society. Like no president before him, he and his team use the tools of direct outreach, coupled with a television and radio infrastructure to be a direct voice to the people, telling them what they want to hear or feel at the expense of the truth. Trump has exploited the fact that the gatekeepers have fallen, and has used his stature to position himself as the truth teller in chief.

Trump knows, for instance, that the public are not experts

---

* Louis Jacobson and Nadia Pflaum, "Trump Tweaks Talking Point About U.S. Being One of the Highest-Taxed Nations, But It's Still Flawed," PolitiFact, July 22, 2016, http://www.politifact.com/truth-o-meter/statements/2016/jul/22/donald-trump/trumps-claim-us-taxes-tweaked/#.

on Defense Department procurement savings, the Guantánamo release process, or international taxes. This is why he
can state that he was able to negotiate $600 million in savings
on F-35 fighter jets, when in reality those cost savings were
negotiated before he took office.* He can boldly proclaim that
"122 vicious prisoners, released by the Obama administration
from Gitmo, have returned to the battlefield," when the truth
is that 113 of them were released under George W. Bush, not
Obama.† He has repeatedly said too that "we are *the* highest-
taxed nation in the world," when the nonpartisan Pew Re-
search Center has consistently noted that American taxes are
below average relative to other developed countries.‡ While
these issues in and of themselves aren't game changers, they
are a vivid reminder that even the most demonstrably false
statements can ring true for those who want them to be.
And when policies or pronouncements that are unequivocally
false are made true, it reinforces the notion that nothing is
out of bounds. It highlights the choice we face as American
people: do we accept that some things are true regardless of
how they make us feel, or do we accept that there can be multiple truths—"alternative facts" with no bearing on reality
whatsoever?

---

* Michelle Y. H. Lee, "Trump's Claim Taking Credit for Cutting $600 Mil-
lion from the F-35 Program," *Washington Post*, January 31, 2017.
† Charlie Savage, "Fact Check: Trump Is Wrong About Guantánamo Detain-
ees," *New York Times*, March 7, 2017.
‡ Jacobson and Pflaum, "Trump Tweaks Talking Point."

Under this president, we have endured an administration repeatedly and deliberately lying to the American people. To Trump, the narrative is always subordinate to the ideas being conveyed, and he will use any combination of facts and lies to anchor an idea. And he traffics in exclusion, employing racism, xenophobia, misogyny, and white supremacy with a flagrancy not seen in recent memory. Whenever he references Obama, he is always suggesting that he has done better, already, than the black man who preceded him, as with the Defense Department procurement issue and the Guantánamo releases, despite them being lies. Whenever he mentions Chicago, he is actively linking danger and the need for increased law enforcement with the presence of black bodies.

Trump aims to distance us so intensely from the facts that in our attempts to find the truth, fatigue besets us. The daily task of truth finding is one that is often too much to engage in at the level that is now necessary. And so people accept statements as true until proven otherwise. By the time a false narrative has been identified as such, it has traveled far and wide. Trump's strategy is to keep you on the defense, spending more time rebutting his lies than developing a plan to actually address his proposals and policies. He seems to have understood, quicker than the media or the broader public, that his base would reframe bold lies as all-too-rare moments of candid honesty in a corrupt political sphere. That they would read his racism as national pride; his sexism as just the normal behavior of powerful men; and his hypocrisy as the cost of being a businessman. It is the ease with which Trump lies with no semblance of self-inquiry or shame that is perhaps the most unsettling thing about him and his team. His very political ascendancy began with him telling a racist story that turned into the birther movement.*

We cannot forget that the media consistently gave platforms to Trump's stories, only now realizing that they also gave a platform to the ideas that those stories carried. His rise is a case study in what happens when the media is controlled by those who have rarely, if ever, been victims of racism, xenophobia, misogyny, and white supremacy; his ideas weren't personally dangerous to them, and so they gave him a platform. In some ways, they are still complicit, even now, by pushing a soul-searching narrative for Democrats, suggesting that the party fundamentally misread the electorate while seeming to ignore the fact that Clinton won the popular vote by over 3 million votes, and that the margin of victory amounted to less than 100,000 votes spread out over a few key states.

They seem to simultaneously suggest that Trump was addressing the needs of the electorate and that Democrats are mistaken in their priorities. This is not to say that reflection and course correction are not necessary, but here the media is

---

* As the claims of Obama's illegitimacy were finally leaving the public conversation, Trump became their chief spokesman, reigniting them with fresh vigor.

complicit in pushing the narrative that somehow Clinton's inherent weaknesses, coupled with Trump's lies, manipulations, and overt appeals to racist and nationalist undercurrents, should lead Democrats to fundamentally reassess their policies, practices, and relationship with key voting blocs, as though it's time to clean house. That in a sense, she should have done more of what Trump did. For instance, that instead of apologizing for her "deplorables" comment, she should have doubled down. Or that she should've fomented division, demonized Trump supporters, and appealed to the most base instincts of her most ardent supporters. Even the Russian influence wasn't taken seriously until recently.

If you've ever caught a liar lying and tried to ask them a direct question, they have likely responded with a story. Liars are master storytellers. It's their power. They know that ideas travel in stories. We have a moral obligation to track and respond to lies. Indeed, in the face of false narratives we must always respond, because not to reply is to allow them to continue to permeate hearts and minds.

IF TRUMP'S FALSE NARRATIVES reinforce the importance of constantly pushing back, the case of Dylann Roof reinforces the understanding that language itself serves both in determining and promoting the false narrative.

It is perhaps our arrogance that leads us to believe that we shape language, rather than the reality that language shapes us too. The stories we tell about perpetrators of violence, especially racial violence, function as their own type of power. Consider how the media covered Dylann Roof.

On a Sunday evening in June 2015, white supremacist Dylann Roof opened fire in the basement of the historically black Emanuel African Methodist Episcopal Church in Charleston, South Carolina, killing nine parishioners. "I chose Charleston because it is most [*sic*] historic city in my state, and at one time had the highest ratio of blacks to Whites in the country," read a line from Roof's racist manifesto, which was presented as evidence against him during his trial. He continued:

> We have no skinheads, no real KKK, and no one doing anything but talking on the internet. Well someone has to have the bravery to take it to the real world, and I guess that has to be me. . . . Negroes have lower IQs, lower impulse control, and higher testosterone levels in generals [*sic*]. These three things alone are a recipe for violent behavior.

Roof is echoing the conclusions of scientific racism, made popular by books like *The Bell Curve*, despite being disproven time and again.

The US Code of Federal Regulations defines terrorism as

"the unlawful use of force and violence against persons or property to intimidate or coerce a government, the civilian population, or any segment thereof, in furtherance of political or social objectives." Dylann Roof was neither called a terrorist in the media nor was he charged with terrorism. Why? It would seem that white supremacy is not a political or social objective of the dominant culture.

Language is the first act. It distributes and redistributes power. It carries the kernel of the ideas that shape how we think about the world. The dominant culture—that is, white people—suppressed the notion of a white terrorist because it is impossible to conceive of whiteness as evil, a space decidedly reserved for black and brown people.

In a recent interview, Allison Williams, the actress who played Rose, a twentysomething daughter in the movie *Get Out*, spoke of surprising interactions she kept having with people reacting to the movie. Her character is charged with luring black people to her family's home in the woods to be hypnotized and auctioned off to a group of older white buyers. Williams revealed that white people often ask her if *her* character was hypnotized, to which she replies, "No! She's *just evil*. How hard is that to accept? She's just bad. We gave you *so many ways* to know that she's bad! She has photos of people's lives she ended behind her! The *minute she can*, she hangs them back up on the wall behind her. That's so crazy! And they're still like, 'But maybe she's also a victim?' and I'm like,

'NO! No!' And I will say, that it is one-hundred percent white people that say that to me."*

White people as a group cannot be thought of as evil or as executors of terror. Invocations of violence, terrorism, crime, and the like are all deeply connected to nonwhite groups. White is the default of what one thinks of when they think of human. So to call them bad would be, I suppose, to suggest that humanity itself is bad. It's a popular idiom that when people of color commit crimes, it's considered pathology, and when white people do it, it's the errant actions of individual actors. In order to preserve this lie, terrorists like Dylann Roof, and whiteness writ large, benefit from being called anything but the precise term that holds them accountable.

Post-truth culture, in which the emotionally resonant stories outweigh true stories, exists in more than our formal political sphere or the media. It exists in the fabric of many of our online and offline communities as well. It is a culture that would render objective facts as mere interpretations, critiques.

But how did we get here? It's one thing to dispute obvious untruths—arguments, policies, strategies that are built on a disregard for the truth or a knowing acceptance of a lie—these things we know to be problematic. And the call to address the

---

* Anne Branigin. "Why 2017 Was the Year of Rose Armitage." *The Root*, December 24, 2017, https://www.theroot.com/why-2017-was-the-year-of-rose -armitage-1821137750.

willful manipulation of language that both reveals and props up white supremacy seems an equally straightforward priority. But in this post-truth moment, we are also experiencing the real-time construction of truth; we are participating in the formation of new ways of being in the world. When we tell our history, we are telling our truth—sometimes this truth may mirror an objective reality; other times it's more subjective, the reality we *think* we experienced. These collections of words are constructed narratives, some more complicated than others. I think that often the most complicated narratives tend to be collapsed into myths—part fact, part fiction. These myths have traditionally helped us make sense of the world, pass on learning, and reinforce virtues we hold in high esteem.

Yet in this moment we're seeing the messy construction of truths in real time, the building of narratives, and the telling of myths around events that hold important meaning in and of themselves and that also serve as launch points of possibility for individuals both now and in the future. And so we must now grapple with which version of the truth we want to elevate, and the degree to which our truth should align more with facts or the good story.

Details matter. When we write history, we must never cede the reality of what transpired to partial truths, even if what we gain is the more palatable story—indeed, especially when that is the case. We must bring every narrative to its greatest alignment with the truth, for when we fail to do so, we invite manipulation and erasure. And in this current moment, which builds on the rich history of the civil rights movement, we have only to look back to see this narrative making, and the consequences of it, in action.

Bayard Rustin, the architect of nonviolent resistance as the primary strategy during the civil rights movement and an adviser to Dr. Martin Luther King Jr., was exiled from the mainstream organizing community because he was an openly gay black man. In a 1987 interview, George Chauncey Jr. asked Bayard Rustin how his sexuality affected his work in the civil rights movement, to which Rustin responded:

> There is no question in my mind that there was considerable prejudice amongst a number of people I worked with. But of course they would never admit they were prejudiced. They would say they were afraid that it might hurt the movement. The fact of the matter is, it was already known, it was nothing to hide. You can't hurt the movement unless you have something to reveal.*

Silence as an act of solidarity, they said. Telling the truth about his identity might do damage, they warned. We can acknowledge that attitudes and perceptions related to sexuality and identity have changed since then, and that to some, this type of

---

* Devon W. Carbado and Don Weise, eds. *Time on Two Crosses: The Writings of Bayard Rustin*, 2nd ed. Jersey City, NJ: Cleis Press, 2015.

compromise may have been justified in the context of the broader change that they were seeking. The argument for this approach has a certain simple logic: since the Civil Rights Act passed, we can look back on these strategies as necessary compromises. But Rustin reminds us that the only threat to movement work would be the withholding of information that could then be revealed, that the truth is its own power. And that the passing of the Civil Rights Act resulted less in a more just future than a more nuanced oppression. One can only wonder how strong, durable, and impactful the movement could have been if it had been a place where the freedom that was advocated for included as an explicit, unabashed goal the empowerment of black men *and* women regardless of creed, origin, or sexuality. Like Colvin's and Robinson's, Rustin's story is a missing story.

When it comes to establishing the truth, we often rush toward the simplified version at the expense of the more complicated, more nuanced narrative. It is one thing to have a more accessible narrative that is a derivative of a more nuanced narrative. It is another thing entirely to replace a nuanced narrative with a more accessible one.

I've always thought of Twitter as the friend that's always awake. It was, and is, a platform that allowed us a way to record and bear witness to our own lives and story in real time and with each other. Often, in the streets, I was experiencing things that I needed to process with others, but there wasn't always someone near for me to connect with. But Twitter, and social media more broadly, changed all of that. Like an ever present friend, I was always able to connect to a larger community and, as important, a larger black community. Black Twitter is as organized and powerful as any offline community, with its own norms, practices, style, and flow. In some ways, Black Twitter has amplified the voice of the individual, always reminding each individual that she exists within a larger whole.

I had eight hundred Twitter followers when the protests began. I was focused on being in the streets, assisting in the planning of actions, and documenting the reality of the protests from the on-the-ground perspective in real time. I started a newsletter in August 2014 that initially had two hundred subscribers and over time grew to over twenty thousand subscribers. With the partnership of Brittany Packnett and Johnetta Elzie, it became a hub for information about events and meetings and news going out on a daily basis in the fall of 2014.

Years before any of us would take to the streets, a college professor was affirming the importance of our lives. In August 2012, Marcus Anthony Hunter, a gay black man, and now the chair of African American Studies at UCLA, was studying black migration. As a professor he studies cities, and he was thinking of a way to challenge his students and others to think about blackness as defined not only by skin color but also by our relationship to and away from power, and to realize that when we consider blackness in that sense, we find that most people are politically black. Over time he had come into an awareness of an irrefutable truth: that black migration and movement is the defining characteristic of growth in cities and always has been—that what black lives choose to do matters significantly. And on August 20, 2012, he fired off a tweet: "check out amazing articles by @jean23bean and aldon morris new ed of @contextsmag #blacklivesmatter."

It was the first time that assemblage of words would ever be used on Twitter, and months later it would take on a life all its own.

FERGUSON WAS A PHENOMENON. It was neither the logical nor inevitable conclusion of a particular wave of organizing or organization, nor the result of a small set of people gathering to start a movement. The truth of that phenomenon, how it started, what galvanized it, what sustained it, why it mattered to the world, and what its legacy is—those stories are finally being told now, by the people who lived them.

The movement was born from the collective energy of a people, not at the direction of a small set of leaders. In the ten days after Mike Brown's death, there were solidarity protests in over forty cities. And on August 14, five days after Mike Brown had been killed, the National Moment of Silence was held in 119 cities worldwide. Inspired by those protesters in St. Louis who came out on August 9 and never turned back, a movement was born and spread across the country.

The suggestion that national organizations came to Ferguson and St. Louis to essentially save the protesters by providing order and direction is dismissive of all the people who did the work of sustaining the longest domestic racial-justice protest in American history—longer than even the Montgomery bus boycott, which was the last protest to hold this distinction. It is true that many national organizations provided support, assisted with strategy, and created access to resources once the protests were under way. But the protests were organic; that was their strength and what created their staying power. Like Jo Ann Robinson and the flyers, in the absence of one organization or set of leaders to save everyone, the people themselves stepped up individually and collectively to birth, nurture, and sustain the movement.

Hashtags are like digital paper clips—and #BlackLives Matter was a crisp clarion call, allowing for increased solidarity and for a common language to describe the protests that were sweeping the country, originating with those in Ferguson, Missouri. But the protests began with #Ferguson organically becoming the rallying cry and call to action. The study "Beyond the Hashtags," published by the Center for Media & Social Impact at American University's School of Communication, reviewed every tweet from June 1, 2014, to May 31, 2015, and noted that the most used hashtags during that time were #Ferguson (21,626,901), #MikeBrown (9,360,239), and then #BlackLivesMatter (4,312,599).* The study helped

---

* Deen Freelon, Charlton D. McIlwain, and Meredith D. Clark. "Beyond the Hashtags: #Ferguson, #Blacklivesmatter, and the Online Struggle for Offline Justice," February 29, 2016, http://cmsimpact.org/resource/beyond-hashtags -ferguson-blacklivesmatter-online-struggle-offline-justice/.

map when #BlackLivesMatter broke through to gain the widespread appeal that it has now, specifically highlighting November 24, 2014, the day of the nonindictment of Darren Wilson, the officer who killed Mike Brown, as the first day that the hashtag achieved mass appeal.

I remember the week that we decided to start transitioning from #Ferguson to #BlackLivesMatter as a key tag for our tweets. The trolls, the coordinated online harassment accounts, had begun to flood #Ferguson, and we also needed a hashtag that would be more inclusive of the other cities in protest. The study also noted that "while social media may have played a critical role in helping activists push police violence to the forefront of public consciousness, this was by no means an automatic process. The mere presence of articles about police killings on social media was not enough: a critical mass of concerned parties had to decide to aggregate their anger into a movement." The authors are right—Twitter was an important vehicle because it amplified the work on the ground and allowed us to be truth tellers about our experience.

I never imagined that a story of the "founding" would emerge or that there would be an attempt to define a set of people as the "founders" of the movement. That some are labeled as such and accept it surprises me. That the founding is credited to me and others despite our making no claim to and actively rejecting the title of "founder" makes me realize that the easy-to-understand story is more palatable than the complicated reality. The founders of the movement were the protesters in the streets.

We were called to the street because of Mike Brown's death, and the beauty of it was that all were welcome—anyone ready to do the work of fighting for justice and accountability. You did not need to pledge allegiance to an organization or have a special degree, certification, or training; you just needed to be ready to do whatever work was necessary. Because no organization started this movement, and no organization sustained this movement.

In retrospect, we can name why Rosa Parks was chosen and not Claudette Colvin. That does not render Rosa's sacrifice unimportant—it does, though, mean our story was only half told. It is because of respectability politics. When we look back, we can name why Jo Ann Robinson was erased, because in a patriarchal society power could not be seen to rest with a woman in this way. It is clear now too that Bayard Rustin was shifted away because of a combination of homophobia and respectability politics. This is something I feel we all have an obligation to disrupt to the best of our abilities by telling the truth about the contributions—of labor and thought—of those in the queer community and of women.

My hope is it will not take decades for us to investigate why it was useful to erase Marcus Anthony Hunter from his labor and thought. The consequences of acquiescing to these myths are real. When we erase Marcus, we lose an understanding of the origin of a phrase that has helped steer an international conversation, and we re-create the patterns of erasure that we work intentionally to disrupt in our work every day. When we say that an organization birthed a movement we send signals, intentionally or unintentionally, that we need to wait for a corps to create the catalyst for change—and we erase thousands of nameless people who sacrificed everything for the movement we see today. We can, and must, develop a deeper ability to describe the phenomena of collective action that accounts for the contributions of the many without falling into the trap of a hierarchy as an organizing structure.

We fight these acts of erasure because they reduce our collective power and the strength of the movement. We are stronger, more capable of achieving our aims, when we tell the full truth, even if it is a more complicated narrative than the half-truth, even if it is a simpler narrative. We can simultaneously acknowledge the work of those who have chosen to lead within organizations focused on justice work, just as we can celebrate the roles of all the people who came out, night after night, as citizens ready to be a part of something bigger than themselves, because they knew that their city needed them. We can do this without allowing our bias toward organizations to erase the labor and contributions of people who might not have access to platforms but who often have done the heaviest and hardest lifting. These truths can coexist alongside the truth that the movement itself was born in the streets and sustained over time through the collective actions of organizations, informal groups, collections of friends, and individuals. We can celebrate the original author of the hashtag, and its intended meaning, without diminishing the role of the hashtag as a rallying point for this renewed focus on freedom and justice.

This matters because our stories shape what we believe to be possible. Our stories inspire. Every activist should revel in her ability to take a stand like Claudette Colvin. Every person who sees an injustice should feel empowered to change history like Jo Ann Robinson. And every person—man, woman, or child—should realize that they can join a movement through organizations or through the power of a phone call to a legislator, and they can start a movement by building community in the streets, without having to wait for an organizer. We know that we can make our signs. We know that we can be present in any space. We know that we don't always need a bullhorn to make our voices heard.

I now understand that history is usually a series of the small, repeated acts of individuals or groups that have impact. Movements are an ecosystem of actions, rarely ever islands of singular leadership. In remembering the displaced narratives of Claudette Colvin, Jo Ann Robinson, and Bayard Rustin, I have begun to think more about narrative sacrifice, about the missing stories, the stories withheld by choice and design. I have also begun to think more deeply about the power and impact of the stories that *are* told and about the language used to tell them—about those who participate in false narratives to serve political aims, those who use language as a shield from inquiry, and those whose tales become a game of hide-and-seek with the truth.

TEN

Out of
the Quiet

*The difference between
a garden and a graveyard
is only what we choose
to put in the ground.*

—RUDY FRANCISCO

S ometimes, when you don't see yourself in the world, you start to think that you don't exist.

I now realize that I saw brotherhood and I saw lust, but I never saw romance between men in real life or on TV before I was an adult. I never saw people my age talking about desire beyond the binary, never experienced pleasure without sneaking. It was not seeing myself in the world that taught me the timidity that it would take until adulthood to break; it was the absence that I felt in this larger world that taught me that quiet would keep me alive, keep me loved, and keep me sane. But I did not know then the cost of the quiet. I did not know that the quiet is a thief, that it steals the potential for joy, for power, for freedom. And like most thieves, it works so that you don't realize you've been robbed until what you once had is already gone. Or perhaps it steals away the possibility of things that you deserved, wanted, expected.

In its best form, art can be a mirror and a window, helping us to better see ourselves and to imagine new possibilities. But what happens when the mirror returns a reflection that doesn't look like the you that you know yourself to be? Or when the window seemingly isn't meant to be opened in the first place?

When I think about the quiet, I think about the places where we've been told that we're not supposed to make a lot of noise, the places where we've been told that the only way to achieve, progress, succeed, is to work in silence. And for so many of us, *the world* is that place.

I think about the quiet instead of "the closet" because I've never hidden any part of myself from myself or from others, and the closet seems to imply some form of hiding. And when I think about being in the closet, I think of being there alone. But there are many people raised in the quiet, still in the quiet, stuck in the quiet, together. And they don't always know that they're not alone, even if it feels like they are. I was never hiding, as the image of the closet implies. But I grew up quieter about the parts of myself that I didn't think anyone would love, the parts that I had never seen loved in others, the parts that might put me in danger if they were seen and heard as publicly as every other part of me. Quieter, that is; not silent.

When I think about the quiet, the image of a library comes to mind—the place where supposedly you can't learn if there's noise, a place of exploration that says *don't speak*. But there are always people whispering and passing notes in the library, always people finding ways to have a voice despite the rules, always people coming out of the quiet. The silence is enforced not just by the obvious presence of the rules but also by the collective self-policing that we learn from those around us. That is, until someone starts to speak, emboldening others to do the same. And then you realize that there's a way to talk, to be, that allows you to say what you need to say, that adds and does not subtract from the space and people around you, that even helps the people who didn't know to ask for help too.

I did not lose my voice in the quiet, but some do. I was young when I learned how to use silence as a weapon, as a tool, as a blanket, as a handkerchief, as a friend. I realized that trauma and pain could outrun me and that fear is often a bully.

When the silence came to suffocate me, I stood still.

I remember the first time like it was yesterday. I remember being on the floor, about to go to sleep. It was nighttime. My sister was sleeping on the couch, but there wasn't enough couch for both of us. Being the boy, I got the floor, which I didn't necessarily mind. We had just installed new carpet at our house, and I loved napping on the floor there. But we were at my father's girlfriend's house on this night.

I remember telling my father that I didn't want to have to sleep on the floor with his girlfriend's nephew. I didn't have the language to explain it then; I didn't have the words to express my hesitation when I was seven, on that night, on the floor, in her house. But I remember saying that I didn't want to have to sleep on the floor with him. In the end, I was told to go to sleep.

This was the first night that he made me touch him. It wasn't the last night. It happened in many houses, in many places, over a span of a few years. I've largely moved those memories to different places, places harder to access, harder to recall, places beyond my easy grasp. It became too much to remember them every day because I still had to be in those places, even if he wasn't there. And I didn't want to think of him every time I walked into my bedroom, or any of the other rooms in our house. Because in some sense, it felt like he was always there. Well, until I decided to move those memories to a place I wouldn't reach anymore.

One night, while I was at my grandmother's house, I went downstairs to the kitchen and I called my father. I had to be quiet because the staircase at her house creaks, and my uncle lives in the basement right off the kitchen. He answered. I just felt like I couldn't hold it in any longer. It was eating away at me to not tell someone, anyone. I cried and told him that X made me touch him. I was eleven. He told me that he'd come in the morning, we'd talk about it, and that he'd help fix this. That I should go back to sleep and that we'd keep this between us for now.

He came in the morning. We talked about it. And two weeks later, I started therapy. As an adult, I can say that I am happy that X remained alive after my father found out. There was no need to have my pain cause more pain.

I remember my first therapy session. The therapist just didn't get it. I remember it like it was yesterday. I felt like I was talking to someone who didn't understand and simply couldn't help me process what had happened so that I could move on and grow. Instead she wanted me to keep explaining and describing everything. I'd spent years not speaking about it, I'd replayed scenarios in my head, and I'd thought about a life where it didn't haunt me. I needed tools beyond recollection. After my second session, I told my father that I didn't need to go to therapy anymore and that I'd be okay.

In hindsight, it wasn't that I didn't need therapy, but rather that so much time had passed between the violations and me discussing them that I had already processed much of my emotions. I needed space to wrestle with how to keep living, and this therapist wasn't equipped to provide that. We don't give young people enough credit for being able to make sense of the world around them, to take things in and let things out, to be shaped and to shape the world around them. I needed something beyond the skill set of that therapist then. We did not have other options, though—we'd kept the abuse a secret from everyone but TeRay, and we didn't want to risk exposure by searching for a new therapist. And so with nowhere else to turn, I went inward.

It was in running from the memories of the pain that I

entered the quiet for the first time. I learned how to use silence then, as a seven-, eight-, nine-, ten-, and eleven-year-old. I learned how to smile and respond when an aunt or uncle would ask me during one of those national weeks about sexual assault if anyone had ever touched me. I learned that I could do and say just enough to get the adults around me to create their own narratives from the bits and pieces I would provide, all the while masking my shame and guilt. I learned how to hide while looking like I was fully present, how to become small in ways that only I knew while ensuring that others would read my behavior as introversion. I learned how to withhold information from the people closest to me, how to appear calm and composed when inside I was burning.

I'd made the commitment soon after therapy that I would not kill myself, ever. I think that it was more practical than anything. We were raised by my great-grandmother and father then. And while my great-grandmother was loving to me, she was hard on my sister in the way that old women raised in a different generation had unreasonable expectations for little black girls. She didn't like that TeRay whistled, or liked wearing pants, or that she played softball. To Nanny, TeRay was never being enough of a lady, even when we were quite young. I barely liked to leave the two of them alone together in the house, and I couldn't imagine leaving the world with them permanently together. I didn't know if my sister would survive her.

I remember the day that I chose not to kill myself, because it was the same day that I decided not to nap in closets anymore—something that I used to do so that my family would think that I'd run away and disappeared forever. When that phase ended, I told myself that I would sit in the pain from there on out. I would let it wash over me, let it surround me, envelop me, let it get as close as it wanted to. And that I would look it in the face. I had run from all those memories of him touching me. I was tired of running.

When the silence came to suffocate me, I stood still. I stood still to show the silence that it would not push me any longer—that it would not win, not this time. But I had run long enough that I learned its tricks, and though I wanted to forget them, I don't think you ever unlearn the tools that kept you alive in the moments when life isn't what you wanted.

I didn't realize that I was in the quiet until college, when I saw people my age who weren't there, who were living loudly. I hadn't seen people showing up in the fullness of who they were until then, not truly. As a kid I mostly saw the constraints, the limitations that poverty created, and sometimes glimpses of joy beyond survival broke through. But seeing other people escape its grasp I realized that I too could get out of the quiet. It was not enough to stand up to the silence that tried to suffocate me; I had to learn how to move past it, to let it pass me by, to take those steps and leave it in my shadow.

I learned quickly that this world wanted me to apologize for my desire, for the way my voice did not sound like the men I saw on TV, for the butterflies I got in the presence of men I dated, the men I loved. But we are to apologize for our mistakes and who I am is no mistake. I refuse to apologize for the timbre of my voice, the sway of my gait, the gender of my love. I did not always have the strength to refuse, but the lessons came slowly like the waves on a beach, slowly but surely, and then all at once. It was in the safety of my first kiss that I learned that men's bodies could do more than break me. It was in the gentle power of the last man I loved that I learned that the words of men could find parts of me to build, parts of me to love that I had not always seen as worthwhile or valuable. It was in holding hands, watching TV, and making meals with the small set of men who have ever professed their love—a love that I embraced, believed, and gave back—that I understood the beauty in the mundane parts of love, in the simple quiet, in the hellos and good-byes, and kisses on foreheads instead of lips, in the Post-it notes and voice mails. I had to learn all of these things in real life, because I never saw them in the imagined worlds of TV or movies or cartoons. It was work to learn a love that made me less an object of desire and more a partner in a shared space.

I am a man too, I reminded myself. But my masculinity did not grow in gyms, or on fields, or in the bedrooms of women. I had to learn that men are many things beyond those that we see in the media. There was a period when I didn't like looking into mirrors in public. There was always one mirror at the house that I would tell people was my favorite mirror, the only mirror that I trusted. But the person I saw in those mirrors in public reminded me of how displaced I often felt, and it was too much of a burden to be displaced in public. I could manage displacement at home. But now mirrors don't bother me. I had to learn that gay black men can be gay and black and men at the same time. I realize that there are people still learning this today.

I am a man who loves men, living in a body that so much of the world has been taught to hate. But I have found communities of men like me, ready, able, and willing to live as boldly as possible; ready to claim voice, and space, and power, because they know that their lives deserve it. I spent so much of my time fighting for justice in a macro sense that I didn't realize that I had not yet understood justice personally—that I too should be able to live in the fullness of who I am every day without threat and with the ability to prosper. I had to challenge people around me who demanded otherwise from me. It was this challenge that led me to tweet, "If your love requires that I hide parts of who I am, then you don't love me. Love is never a request for silence." I realized that so many people who had ostensibly been good to me in my life had been asking me to be silent about parts of me, especially me being gay. And that's not love.

I like to think that having to navigate so much complexity, constantly fumbling around in uncertain spaces, is what helped me in those early days of protest. I remember standing at the intersection across from MoKaBe's, the coffeehouse that became a meeting spot for activists when we were in St. Louis City. Hours later, a group of us would be inside as the police took aim at all the open doors and windows and fired tear gas at us. But before taking refuge in the coffeehouse, we'd been assembled out front. The police had split our large group into four separate groups, and I'd been separated from the people I'd come with. I recognized the protesters around me—the result of many nights in the streets together—even if I didn't know their names. And then I watched with mild surprise as someone in front of me yelled to the police, "You fucking faggots!" And as he turned around to rejoin the group of protesters, another guy looked at him and said, "Man, that offended me." And the guy who'd yelled the words apologized, said he didn't mean to be offensive, and then they both dissolved into the crowd.

This all happened in a few moments and amid the chaos in the middle of the street. I'll never forget it. It was in Shaw, a neighborhood of St. Louis, in the early months of the protests, after the killing of VonDerrit Myers. And it felt like something was changing about the way that we were starting to build community, and certainly the ways in which we were starting to think about identity. I'd become accustomed to homophobia and hadn't any reason to believe that it was ebbing—until the protests began. Suddenly, we were having these public conversations about things that we'd only discussed privately, if at all. So to see a stranger confront another stranger about his homophobia as we were working to build a community together stood out. And now I realize that it was only just the beginning.

I knew even then that we were building something magical. We were, all of us, building something that would be bigger than our opposition to the police, bigger than our calls for accountability or our sprints to outrun tear gas and rubber bullets. I realized in that moment that in the process of challenging a system that was killing us, we were learning to stand up to the silence that also tried to kill us, and that it was perhaps this that would be the lasting success of the protests at the personal level for each of us.

The narrative of the civil rights movement is often centered around the narratives of men. In those early days, it seemed as if men were determined to exert their own sense of primacy to this movement. Sexism and misogyny were rampant: men told women that it was too dangerous for them to be outside, men ensured that they led the marches and actions, and men talked over women at the meetings. But those attempts at silencing the women were met with their own sort of resistance. Women led marches and planned actions. Their voices explained and unpacked what was unfolding. Black women were the first people I organized with in St. Louis: Brittany Packnett, Johnetta Elzie, Alexis Templeton, Kayla Reed. And other women like Elizabeth Vega, Pastor Traci Blackmon, and Pastor Renita Lamkin were pivotal influencers and leaders. Black women have long been an incredible force in the work. We know there would not have been a civil rights movement without the work of black women or queer folks, though they were not recognized in their time. And likewise, this movement would not exist without the work of black women and queer folk, who, unlike before, are not being glossed over. They refuse to be content to work in the quiet.

But we weren't having conversations about identity then. Some of that was practical—the police were so wild that all of our collective energy was focused on withstanding them. It became clear, though, because we were forming friendships so quickly and in the midst of chaos, that we'd need to have these conversations in a hurry. So we started talking. Constructing a new lexicon together was both important and necessary, because the only way we'd learn to build a welcoming community was by learning how to talk to one another, especially about who we were.

When we finally had the space to publicly engage with topics concerning identity—topics like queerness, masculinity, feminism—the conversations were hard. In life outside the classroom, or outside the school, I have observed so few opportunities to engage with identity. Though they be messy, these are yet necessary conversations to have. One's identity doesn't just live within them alone, but exists, rightly or wrongly, in relation to others. When we experience things together, it is important that we process them together too, and that we consider both the community we inherited and the community we want to create.

Many of the relationships built in those days of protest are versions of trauma bonding—we met and became close with each other in the midst of shared pain, because of shared pain, or in attempting to avoid pain, together. We met each other as we fought, not the other way around.

Relationships built in and around trauma require that we are even more attentive to explicitly processing the future that we want to build and the barriers that have kept that world from existing; otherwise we can find ourselves re-creating or re-producing conflict in order to have a foundation on which to bond. Friendship and love cannot thrive when trapped in trauma. I've found that we were fighting for a larger freedom without acknowledging the need for an ethic of freedom and liberation in our interpersonal relationships.

See, the thing about the quiet is that it doesn't only affect the people stuck in it. It creates a world in which those not in the quiet—generally those in power—believe that they're the only people, that they are the sum total of humanity. The quiet creates a world in which people can say and do things that hurt those they work with, live with, and seemingly love, without them thinking about it. It is how narratives that do damage continue to travel, to hold power, to move.

In the absence of a space that exists in which you can see yourself, you must create a space that you feel safe in and you must do it in a way that allows you to show up fully, that allows for all of the behaviors, actions, and attitudes that you were quiet about before. And like in the library, when you whisper, other people will hear it and come over; other people will realize that they too can talk.

There are many people with clean hands, but who have

killed—people who have used words like "faggot," "dyke," and "tranny" to destroy lives, to crush spirits, to harm in ways that take a lifetime to heal. And they did not always mean to kill, but they did. Some said they were merely joking, as if words were mere wisps of smoke and not tools of power. Others knew their power and wielded it anyway; they took pride in murder. But our power can never be defined by the things we destroy; it must be, must always be, defined by the things we build. I have seen people indifferent about the lives they've damaged because they fail to understand that destruction is not something to be proud of—that anyone can destroy, but only few can build. I have seen people murder because they have yet to understand that the lives of those they seem to hate have value. And these people, those who kill, don't realize that they are likely to be the victim one day. Indeed, that there will be someone for whom their own identity does not have value, and the weapon their predator employs might not be words but something else, something perhaps even deadlier.

I now realize that gay black men are often meant to adorn, to embellish, to enhance the things around us, but are rarely, if ever, meant to stand on our own. The treatment is akin to the way one regards a nice pair of earrings, an accessory that serves a particular purpose until it doesn't. And this plays out in relationships with men and women, on a loop. To homophobic men, you're never really one of the guys, so the moment conflict arises, you're reminded that you weren't actually welcome in the first place. And to homophobic women, the moment conflict arises, you're reminded that you weren't really one of the girls either. In men, homophobia is often loud; in women, it often is playing softly in the background before it becomes loud. I now know that the pernicious aspect of homophobia, like most things, begins with the ideas, laying the ideological and theoretical foundation that then allows physical violence to manifest.

In activism, I am often asked if I am gay or black first, as if I am not black and gay and male at the same time, all day, every day. The writer Myles Johnson said it best: "Blackness and queerness do not exist in the body separately like oil and water. Blackness and queerness come together like hydrogen and oxygen to make a newer, stronger, and more relentless element."* I am asked if the "gay agenda" has superseded the goal of bringing about justice and equity, as if there aren't gay black people or as if the oppressions aren't connected, interwoven. I encounter homophobic people who are kind to me, who treat me as an exception to their hatred, as if I want to exist as the temporary respite from the terror they inflict in the world so I can be a tool of whatever aims they have in the moment. And sometimes I encounter those who fetishize black masculinity itself, only recognizing stereotypical renderings of black men as desirable, in lust with specific attributes of the black

---

* Myles Johnson. "A Clockwork Trauma." Bitch Media, July 12, 2016, https://www.bitchmedia.org/article/clockwork-trauma-orlando-pulse-shooting-police-violence-intersection-race-queer.

male body, but not in love with blackness or black men. The black male body becomes an object to be consumed, not to be loved; worthy of sex, but not of partnership.

How do the language and actions that reinforce the regressive notions of identity, especially homophobia, emerge? There are four primary ideas that lend themselves to homophobia and that circulate and do damage: first, that the media privileges effeminate gay men over traditionally masculine gay men and are thus contributing to the weakening of masculinity, and in the case of black folks, blackness itself; second, that being gay is inherently a sign of weakness, as if one's strength or commitment to justice is defined by the person one loves; third, that blackness is one's primary identity and that the "gay agenda" is ruining our collective fight for liberation, as if identity is not interwoven and complex; and last, that identity is a choice and we should not highlight trans communities or gay communities because some heterosexual parents don't want their children to "choose" an identity not within the strictures of heterosexuality.

In the media, black people are either entertainers or are still centered on trauma—shown heroically or romantically surviving the impact of trauma or celebrating the survival in the end. It is only recently that shows with majority black casts allow for multidimensional characters to exist as staples and not as mere momentary features. The core of this language that dismisses or defames the complexity of identity is an attempt to advance the idea that there should not be many identities but a singular identity, that the embrace of identities somehow weakens us collectively. It is the same force that whiteness advances and blackness resists. Here it is homophobia. There it is racism. In other places anti-Semitism or Islamophobia.

All of this serves to distract us from engaging with the only true question that matters: do we view ourselves as stronger when we make space on our team for those who didn't think they had a place or not? I will always believe that an embrace of others' identities makes us stronger. The work of justice always begins from a place of disadvantage, a recognition that this country has not yet guaranteed access, equity, and opportunity as we can and should. And the way to transition from disadvantage into advantage is by tapping into the quiet and building a team of those who understand the work.

The challenge is that I know I'm fighting for people who don't think I'm worthy of fighting with. Partly because, I think, so many parts of ourselves are in the quiet in ways that we don't acknowledge, that it's hard to understand the parts of ourselves that share the quiet with parts of others. I've been in spaces where the homophobia is palpable, from men and women. I try to remember that culture doesn't shift as quickly as we always want it to and that no individual carries the burden of being the entrance into the work of justice for everyone. But it's hard to know that one's criticism of me is not rooted in a particular idea I've expressed or a policy position, but in their perception of the politics of my love and my identity.

When those in the quiet come out of it, and come together, the world changes. In many ways, the quiet is not living in an identity and disavowing it, but being alone in it, unsure of what to do there. Over the past four years, I've learned that there are so many people coming out of the quiet, so many people looking for ways to be seen and heard, waiting for others who share the belief that there is power in collective whispers. And it's happening all across the world—all of us tweeting, all of us who thought that we were alone, all of us who thought that our stories about the violence we'd endured would go unheard. Social media became, and is, the place where people come out of the quiet and come together, where the collective power of the whisper is captured, where the silence is rendered into deafening sound. It was on Twitter that we learned to fight erasure. In protest, we became the unerased. Each of us will have to continue to find the people in the quiet and to create space for and with them. Our work as organizers is neither to tell the people whispering in the library to shout, nor is it to tell folks to be quiet—our work is to listen better.

Just because people aren't shouting doesn't mean that they are being silent.

Just because people aren't showing up in the way we expect doesn't mean that they are hiding.

We have to remember that we are all of our identities at once, every time.

ELEVEN

On Organizing

No, I do not weep at the world—
I am too busy sharpening my oyster knife.

—ZORA NEALE HURSTON

I n our first summer in Ferguson, the sweat was almost as endless as our resolve. I was intrigued and relieved when we got word that there would be a training session by a national organizer in a local church. It seemed like a good opportunity both to cool off and to learn. Up until then, we had spent the majority of our time in the street; and when we weren't in the street, we were meeting in small groups to plan actions. There hadn't been any formal training yet. Perhaps, I thought, we would learn the art of organizing.

It was hot in the meeting room at the church too, but still cooler than it was outside. When the organizer arrived, she began by teaching us about power mapping—the skill of identifying the key levers of power in a given context and noting ways to influence and/or challenge them. In a more traditional setting, this may have been an ideal lesson. But we were getting teargassed, pepper sprayed, arrested, and shot at with rubber bullets. We knew who had the power, and it wasn't us. We didn't need to map it.

Looking back, it's clear that we walked into the room that day with the fundamental skills we needed to be effective activists and organizers—and that we'd walked into many rooms with more skills than we thought we had. Sure, we needed to refine them and sharpen them and use them in targeted ways. But when it came to organizing, to coming together to build power in order to collectively confront a problem and then work to solve that problem, it seemed to me that thinking about this activity as a series of tactics that needed to be taught was insufficient. That tactics would be taught suggested a typical top-down model in which an organizing body or institution confers knowledge, gives direction, grants permission. The work of organizing precedes the organizations and it precedes the tactics. Organizing is the act of bringing people together in an effort to harness communal energy to challenge a system or structure to bring about a specific, desired change. From there, the methods and tactics groups employ can vary greatly.

Back then, I thought that we were going to show up and learn the secrets of organizing, that the instructor would introduce us to practices as-yet-unknown to us that would undoubtedly increase our likelihood of achieving our goals. I thought she'd hand us the playbook for organizing. Instead, what we got were a set of tactics and strategies that we couldn't use. They were developed and employed in a time and place wholly different from the context we were in and the things we were experiencing.

Now, this isn't to say that we can't learn from the organizers and activists who have come before us. We can and we must. But I had an epiphany in that room: I realized that there were no secrets, only ideas and tactics that perhaps had not been adapted to a particular moment or were yet to be discovered, and there wasn't a mythical one-size-fits-all playbook that would liberate us. Importantly, what this means is that organizers must employ the tools and tactics that are available. The tactics that were effective in bringing about change in the sixties, seventies, and eighties are well known to all—especially those who oppose them. Indeed, the detractors have had decades to adapt to them. And thus we needed new tactics for a new time. To ignore the role of social media as difference-maker in organizing is perilous. If anything, the most recent election and the manipulation of social media by foreign parties show that the strategies of organizing and influencing are evolving. Knowing this, I was finally free to begin to imagine, and to feel empowered to create new tactics and strategies.

We don't enter spaces empty-handed, like we think we do. And we don't always pay attention to the things we carry, or the things that carry us. For many of us, things like a sense of safety, the people we love, and peace of mind have all been lost. But we did not misplace these things; they were taken from us.

Even so, we are still carrying pieces of all the lost and taken things with us, every day. And we're holding on to other things too—other things that have remained ours, things that give us strength and power and joy. We must take inventory of the things we carry, and no matter how frequently we experience loss, we must resist the urge to forfeit our dreams, our hopes, our lives, in anticipation of having them taken from us.

Baltimore, its own Charm City, taught me how to think about organizing—what it looks like, what it feels like, and why it matters. And from my teenage years on, my understanding of organizing was one that viewed organization and structure as necessary components. The people I'd seen who organized were either members or employees of an existing organization. And there was always a primary vehicle for disseminating the message—a formal campaign, a 501(c)(3), an established, enduring framework.

In school, we were taught about SNCC and SCLC, the power of the black church and historically black colleges and universities as political forces, and the NAACP. I had not imagined a way to organize outside of a traditional structure before. And even when I imagined organizing that wasn't embedded in an organizational structure, it still followed familiar practices and tactics—nonviolence, boycott, Alinsky's principles, and the like.

We have a tendency to frame the activity of building power as something that happens within the aforementioned structures. But if building power is simply about people coming together in an effort to identify and challenge an injustice, and proposing and/or imagining solutions that either mitigate harm or remove the challenge altogether, then the only thing required is people with a shared vision. Indeed, the only constants in organizing are relationships. Everything else is fluid. It is impossible to organize people with whom you have no relationship—impossible to organize people when you have no proximity to the challenges, to the work being addressed. In this same vein, we must remember not to confuse proximity to trauma with proximity to the work. There are many people who have the former and not the latter, for instance. And a person's proximity to trauma does not make their analyses any stronger than another's when they are not informed by an understanding of the actual frameworks and mechanisms of power and of the range of solutions possible.

Part of the work of bringing about the world that we deserve is ensuring that our strategies and tactics grow as we grow, that we continually reflect on how power shifts and how the forces we're up against adapt and respond to the strategies we've employed. And we must use all the tools we have at our disposal. We have now what many activists and organizers before us never had: the internet and social media. And because of this, we can communicate with and mobilize thousands, millions, at once. As Jason Mogus has written, organizing is the act of building power; mobilizing is the act of spending the power you've built.

The lesson I came away with that day in the church was not the lesson I expected to learn, but sometimes you don't know what you don't know, and seeing the blind spot is the best lesson of all.

TWELVE

Letter to
an Activist

*We need, in every community, a group
of angelic troublemakers.*

—BAYARD RUSTIN

S elah, Isaac, and others,

You have more power than you know, more power than they will ever want you to know, and they will spend their lives trying to hide you from yourself. But you have the strength of a people standing beside you. You do not stand in the shadow of those who fought before you; you stand in their glow.

Remember, there is no America without you. This America was built on the backs of the people who died so that you could live, and the other brown peoples who were first displaced. Your claim to this country, to justice, is not merely one of ethics and morality. Your claim to this country is rooted in the reality that you, and the people of whom you belong, have already incurred the highest costs possible for the things you seek, and the time for payment is long overdue.

In fighting to help this country, this world, to be one that is worthy of the beauty of your life, you will undoubtedly experience pain—the normal pain of life and the pain of struggle. But pain is not who you are. You are, and have always been, more than your pain.

I have found that there's a natural progression from thinking that you are the problem to realizing that the problem is rooted in the world and that you are impacted by it. I had to learn that liberation is not the same as struggle. Liberation is about the process of getting to the freedom and justice that our lives deserve. Struggle is how we talk about the act of fighting. They are related but not the same.

Language is often our first act of resistance. It matters how we talk about the work we do; the words we use or the words we create matter to describe the world we live in, the freedom and justice we deserve. It matters not whether you call yourself protesters or organizers, activists or the like. Whatever title you assume, be the people committed to fighting for accountability and justice. Let that be what defines you.

Be mindful not to internalize the ills of the world, but to be able to recognize them and then actively work to disrupt them and undo their damage. You have surely learned things by now that you did not choose to learn: misogyny, homophobia, sexism, and so on. You learned these things because they are often so deeply entrenched in the fabric of culture that you may not always realize that there are alternatives. But there are. And the work of unlearning is almost harder, in some ways, than the work of learning. But you will need to identify these things and unlearn them and help those around you to do the same.

The poet Cleo Wade wrote, "Not every ground is a battleground." We get so used to fighting. We learn the battle so well that it bleeds over into everything. It becomes a hallmark of all of our relationships, even our relationship with ourselves. But not every ground is a battleground.

To the question "What can I do?" I say, I wish there were an easy answer. I know that in order to do this work well, you've got to know an issue. Find an issue or a set of issues and learn them well. It's hard to fight for things you don't understand or for people you don't know. Proximity matters. There's a phrase that I've heard many people weaponize in this work: The people closest to the problem are closest to the solution. In reality, I think the truth is that the people closest to the problem are closest to the problem and that it's impossible to be close to the problem without being close to the solution.

In my hometown, I have seen families impacted by violence support policies against their own interests—policies like mandatory minimums, which we know have no positive impact on the criminal justice system. We need to make sure that we maintain proximity to the work at hand. Too often we confuse proximity to trauma with proximity to work.

And be mindful not to reproduce the same elitism and gatekeeping in the work of social justice that we aim to remove in larger society. The attitude of scarcity and control, of "if you don't do this work with or like me, then you're not real," will never lead to liberation. We have to be open to disagreement in this work. And we need to remember that our ideas can be in conflict without us being in conflict. When we come in conflict with each other, as people, it should only be to defend our core beliefs about everyone's right to show up as full people, every time, in every way.

Do not turn your identities into tombstones; indeed, do not be ashamed of who you are. Our identities are as complex as the world we live in. We have every right to be trans, queer, gay, gender fluid, straight, bi, cis, and be whole and safe and happy and healthy and free. It is not our fault that the world has not moved as quickly to understand the complexity of our identities as we have in understanding the complexity of ourselves, even if it becomes our burden. When we show up in our fullness, we work to create space for those who stand beside us and who will come after us. And it is not always easy to show up fully, just as it is not always easy to stand in the face of adversity. Will you stand if you have to stand alone?

If you are reading this, you have survived. Be ever mindful that this work we engage in is undertaken in memory of those who did not survive, and to ensure that we never have to think about survival as a key axis again.

Our work needs no more martyrs. You can fight these fights and live. You can experience joy and beauty too. If you are not constantly refueling yourself, you will have nothing to pour into this work. If you're ever afraid, you must learn to walk toward the fear.

I wish someone had told me sooner that the best idea doesn't always win, but that the idea that wins is the idea that is reinforced day in, day out, to the point that it becomes second nature. I think that the people we fight against understand this better than the people on our side ever have. I now understand the power of storytelling and how ideas become anchors for actions. Remember, some of the most important things you will do is create entrances and on-ramps for people to be able to understand the work in which you engage so that they can then carry the message of the work and the work itself forward.

It is unlikely that you will be able to win alone. We will need each other if we are to get to a place where we end oppression and create the conditions where we protect that win. We often forget about protecting the wins that we do get, so they can't be rolled back. But protecting the win is perhaps one of the most important parts of all that we do. You will need other people to help you do this work. You did not get here alone. And working with others will be natural in some ways because our issues are linked, not ranked. As you've heard before, when we are free, everyone is free.

Your curiosity will be your biggest weapon. Curiosity is imagination's cousin. When you start to pull back the curtain on the world around you, you start to see that this was built by someone—and that you can be a builder too. Ask all the questions that come to mind. People will want to beat your curiosity out of you, but hold fast.

You never have to defend your rage. You have every right to be angry about the conditions that you were born into. You did not choose this fight; this fight chose you. That we ask for justice and not revenge is a testament to the souls of black folks—that we will not become the people we fight against. Do not let people demand your happiness either. All these things are yours—yours to decide how to put into the world on your own schedule.

I still have more to learn, but I wanted to share the things that I've learned so far about this world, about this work, about myself.

Keep the fight.

DeRay

Acknowledgments

To all the protesters who stood in the streets in those early days, before anyone knew that people all over the world would eventually support us, thank you for reminding me of the power of everyday people coming together to demand something different, of the power of community to create new energy that could be transformative. And to all the protesters who joined in the movement as the work rippled across the world, thank you for heeding the call and helping to build the power necessary to eventually have the impact that we deserve.

I have known many people in my life, but I have had no friend like Donnell Paul O'Callaghan III (Donnie). We have been friends for a decade, beginning in Maine, then working together in New York City, Minneapolis, and Baltimore. He is the brother I never had, the friend one can only hope for, and the confidant and thought-partner who helps to create space where none existed before. There would be no book without Donnie's wisdom and his gifts, and I would not know how to maneuver around and in the written word without his gift for brevity and wit.

Calvin Mckesson, my father, taught me how to love. He taught me that love is not a game of winners and losers, that big hearts can always be bigger, and that sometimes we make sacrifices for the people we love. He also taught me that our gifts always show up when we share—of ourselves, our resources, our time. It is this spirit, in many ways, that pushed me to protest in the first place, this sense of love.

TeRay Ross, my sister, was my first friend, and she taught me how to love in the easy times and the hard times. She has always been a steadying force in my life, present but never overbearing, firm but never heavy-handed, caring but never suffocating. I will always be indebted to her love. And it is a lifetime honor to be the uncle of her children, Selah and Isaac.

I gained a new family in protest, and like all families we have had a range of experiences together. We've had the high highs and the low lows, but we've remained committed to a common purpose in the work that brought us together in the first place. To Brittany Packnett, you were the first person I met in protest and we have been side by side ever since. Your clarity, focus, steadfastness, and resourcefulness shaped so many moments that it would be impossible to recount them all. And your generosity of spirit combined with your sense of faith continue to be a model in my life. Thank you for being a sister and a friend. And thank you (and your mother) for allowing me to sleep on your couch all those late nights, and for being patient with me. I love you.

To Johnetta Elzie, we have been through so much together, both literally and figuratively. In some ways, I don't know if any words will ever convey how close we've become. I still think about all those long nights out in the streets, doing the work that we both felt called to, and I am honored that we got to do it together. Thank you for being friend and family, for pushing when pushing was necessary, for showing me that love can be both a challenge and a call to action, and for keeping a commitment to the truth at the forefront of all this work. And tell your grandparents, aunt, and Tootie thank you for being family too!

To Samuel Sinyangwe, you helped me understand a sense of possible, to see the way the world could be that I didn't know. Every day, I'm in awe of the way your mind works, of your ability to remain positive in the midst of challenges, and of the self-awareness that allows you to course correct when necessary. It has been an honor being a partner in this work and I am proud to call you friend and family.

To Leon Kemp, you were the brother and friend I never thought I'd meet, but then you were there. You've taught me so much about myself, about the world, and about holding true to the commitments that we make, especially in the hardest moments.

To Reggie Cunningham, your sense of resolve has always been a model to me, from those initial nights in Shaw to now, and I am proud to call you a friend.

Acknowledgments

To Kayla Reed, I remember the night you led your first action and I will never forget you finding your power, a gift that I've always known would change the world. I will always be grateful for the time we've spent together and for the way we found joy together, especially in those early days.

To Alexis Templeton, we've had a connection since the first day we met. Thank you for being a friend and creating a space where I've always felt welcomed. I've learned so much from you, about walking into the risk, about self-love and self-care, and about the radical power of honesty.

To Elizabeth Vega and the other activists, for your ingenuity, creativity, and leadership throughout the protests, notably the sit-in at the St. Louis Metro Police Department.

To Cait Hoyt, you believed in this book before almost anybody else and you helped others believe too. Thank you for your willingness to do things differently, to shape and mold it beyond even my hopes, and to be there every step of the way.

In no small way, Georgia Bodnar, my editor at Viking, helped craft this book into something that would flow, would speak, would do work beyond mere storytelling, and I am eternally grateful for her grit, follow-through, sense of possibility, and feedback. If I never see another PDF of her edits, I will die a happy man, but her feedback has only made me, and this book, better.

When I first decided to go to St. Louis, I didn't know where I would stay. I just knew that I was going to go. Jessica Cordova Kramer has been a guardian angel of sorts, always there in the most dire circumstances to help make a way out of no way.

Thank you, Jessica, for connecting me to Brittany on the first day, a day that changed my life.

To Robin Williams Wood and Dr. James Wood, I always talk about you as my second set of parents. But in reality, you are like my parents and best friends and mentors all wrapped up in one. Thank you for loving me from my angsty teenage days to my now less-angsty but still hardheaded adulthood. And thank you for being a resource and helping hand in those moments when I was not as willing to accept help or love or feedback as I could've been. 1104 forever.

To Sharhonda Bossier, you believed in me in moments when I didn't believe in myself, and I will always be indebted to your sense of love, your sheer talent, and your tenacity. I would work with and for you anywhere, anytime. Thank you for being a friend and for modeling a sense of purpose that I had only theretofore read about.

To Barry Mills, I am honored to consider you a friend, mentor, and partner. Thank you for always being there, especially when I needed it and wasn't the most willing to receive feedback. I appreciate you.

To Ivy Blackmore, thank you for opening up your spare bedroom in those early days in St. Louis. You responded to the Facebook post and became a resource right when I needed help the most, and that was invaluable. I don't know what I would have done without you.

To Maggie Sullivan, your leadership forever changed my understanding of my own. You trusted my work, my mind, and my commitment to justice in the most challenging times, and I will always be indebted to the space that you both carved out and defended for me. Thank you, Maggie.

To Miss Margaret, you opened up your home to me on several occasions, making it easier to find a place to sleep given the unpredictability of everything in the initial wave of protests. Thank you for your hospitality and generosity.

To the journalists—Yamiche Alcindor, Wesley Lowery, Ryan Reilly, Matt Pearce, Chris Hayes, Don Lemon, David Carson, and Robert Cohen, thank you for your unwavering commitment to the truth, especially in the early days when people did not believe the protesters. You were there in person, helping to shape a narrative that would change the world.

To the philanthropic, individual, and limited organizational funds—that have not exceeded $140,000 to date—that have allowed us to do this work nimbly and unencumbered from the constraints often associated with large organizational budgets or awards, thank you.

To Frank Chi and Will Donahoe, I feel like I've known you both for a lifetime. Thank you for always being a sounding board and for specializing in making the impossible possible. I hope that we work together for another lifetime, helping to push people beyond even their wildest imaginations.

To Lauren Dorman, you helped us with design when we were just beginning, unclear about the pathway but clear about our big goals. Thank you for being there and for using your gifts to help us access our own.

To Clint Smith III, thank you for being an honest and present friend, helping us all to think more critically about the world around us and more deeply about our own commitments as we live them.

To Reb Z and Heather De Mian, thank you for being truth tellers both in person and digitally. Your live streaming helped create access for people all over the world, and the protests would never have taken the shape they did without your work.

To Yvette Noel-Schure, Sophie Ash, and Lauren Wirtzer Seawood, thank you for believing in my voice and for pushing me to think bigger about how to make an impact. Yvette, thank you for your love and wisdom. Sophie, thank you for your faith and friendship. Lauren, thank you for your loyalty to this work and your loving-kindness.

To Solange Knowles Ferguson and Alan Ferguson, thank you for being there the day I got out of jail in Baton Rouge. I will never forget walking into the house and seeing you both there, present, loving, and ready to help. And thank you both for continuing to use your platforms to amplify the work of protesters across the world.

To Jesse Williams, I'll never forget turning around that night outside of the Ferguson Police Department and seeing you. You've remained as committed from that day forward, and it is an honor to call you a friend and partner in this work.

To Colin Kaepernick, thank you for being a friend and using your platform and your voice to tell the uncomfortable truths that this nation likes to hide from.

To Beyoncé Knowles-Carter, thank you for each of our conversations, your support and the assistance of your team, and the way that you have chosen to share your gift with the world.

Acknowledgments

And to the host of friends, mentors, and colleagues whose counsel, happiness, and friendship at some point over the past four years provided necessary fuel for me in the hardest moments: Travon Free, Dr. Vernon Mitchell, Dr. Brandon Terry, Jack Dorsey, Dr. Sonja Brookins Santelises, Alison Perkins-Cohen, Muhiyidin Moye, the MuckRock team, Rob and Monica Norman, Kate Childs, Darnell Strom, Auriel Brown, Angel Carter, Brianna Richardson, Keith Rose, Alisa Mixon, Jonathan Pulphus, Alisha Sonnier, Kaleb Steele, Alicia Street, Jussie Smollett, Tracee Ellis Ross, Mark Hendrickson, Justin Hansford, and Cleo Wade.

And to the entire team at Viking Books, who broke all the rules in making this book happen and who believed in my story before it ever hit the page, especially Brian Tart, Andrea Schulz, Wendy Wolf, Tess Espinoza, Carlynn Chironna, Gabriel Levinson, Tricia Conley, Alyson D'Amato, Caitlin Noonan, Rebecca Marsh, Olivia Taussig, Theresa Gaffney, Liza Sweeney, Nora Alice Demick, Lydia Hirt, Jason Ramirez, Meighan Cavanaugh, Claire Vaccaro, Linda Friedner, and my copy editor, Jane Cavolina, thank you.